ROYAL COPENHAGEN

ROYAL COPENHAGEN

H.V.F. Winstone

STACEY
INTERNATIONAL

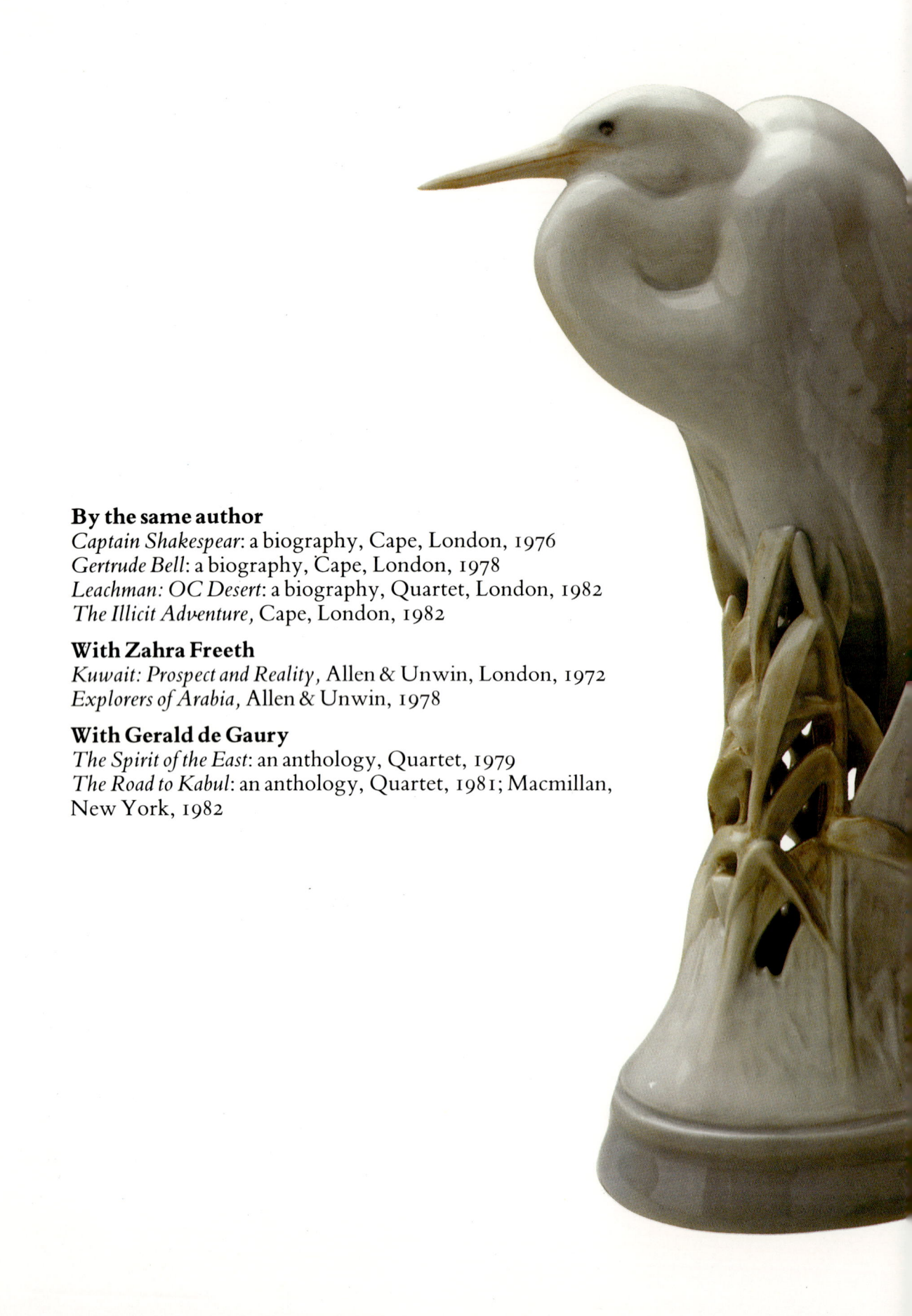

By the same author
Captain Shakespear: a biography, Cape, London, 1976
Gertrude Bell: a biography, Cape, London, 1978
Leachman: OC Desert: a biography, Quartet, London, 1982
The Illicit Adventure, Cape, London, 1982

With Zahra Freeth
Kuwait: Prospect and Reality, Allen & Unwin, London, 1972
Explorers of Arabia, Allen & Unwin, 1978

With Gerald de Gaury
The Spirit of the East: an anthology, Quartet, 1979
The Road to Kabul: an anthology, Quartet, 1981; Macmillan, New York, 1982

For H. A.-J.
A debt of friendship partially repaid

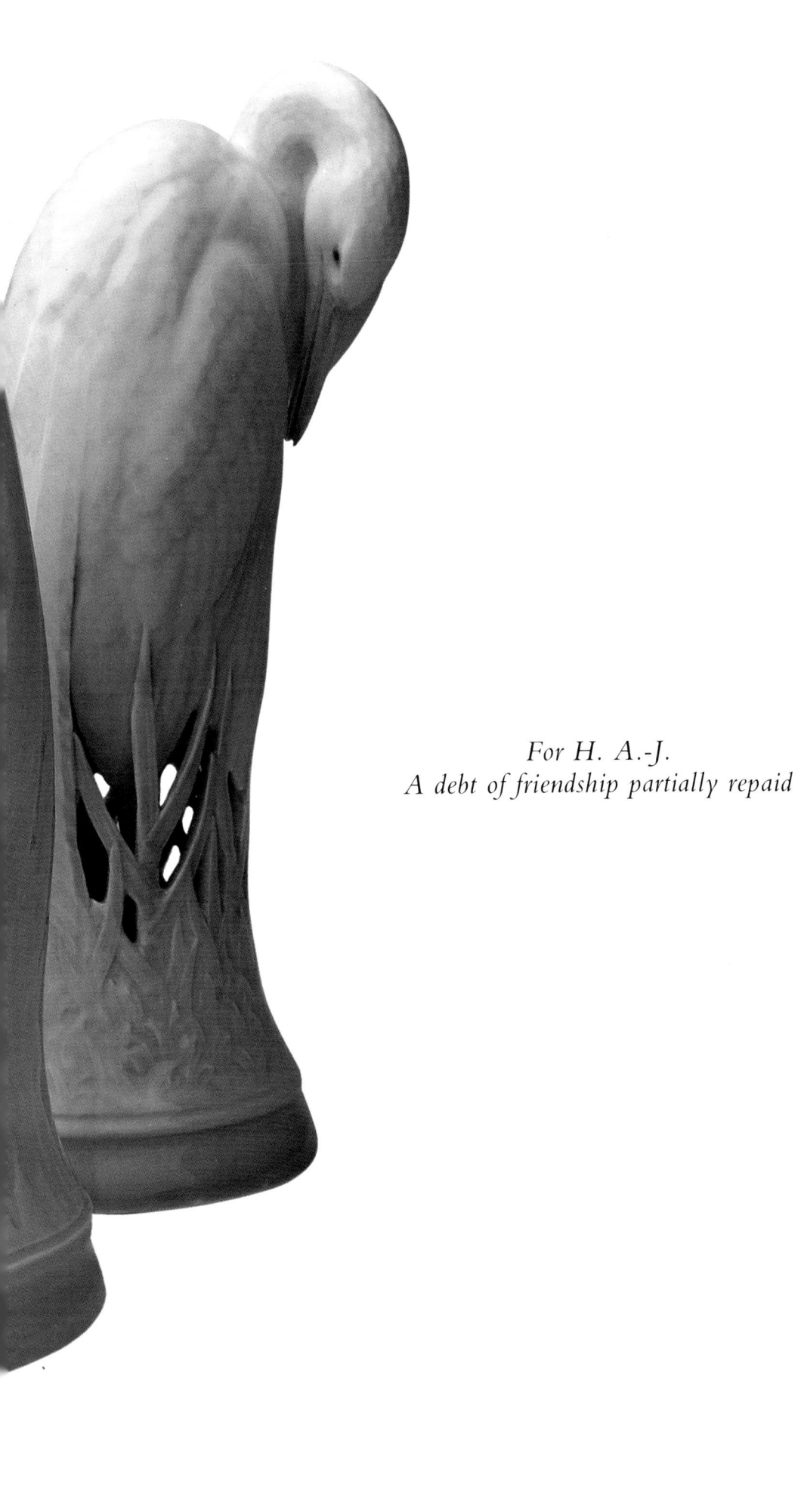

Editorial
John Blackett-Ord
Kenneth Lowther
Sydney Francis

Design
Keith Savage
Morgan C. J. Almeida

Royal Copenhagen
published by Stacey International
128 Kensington Church Street,
London W8 4BH
Telex: 298768 Stacey G

© Victor Winstone 1984

ISBN 0 905743 37 7

All rights reserved. No part of this publication may be reproduced, stored in a retrieval system, or transmitted in any form or by any means, electronic, mechanical, photographic or otherwise, without prior permission of the copyright owner.

Set in Linotronic Bembo by
SX Composing Ltd, Essex, England.
Colour origination by
Hong Kong Graphic Arts Service Centre, Hong Kong.
Printed and bound by
Leefung-Asco Printers Ltd, Hong Kong.

Frontispiece: *Queen Juliane Marie. Modern porcelain version of bust by the sculptor C. F. Stanley, made in 1776.*

Title page: *Pieces from 'Blue Fluted', most renowned of all European blue-painted patterns, sometimes known as the 'Immortelle' or 'Copenhagen' design, dating from c. 1776. Items shown here are from the range created by Arnold Krog in the revival period from 1885, and are in production at the present day.*

Previous page: *Herons, modelled by Theodor Madsen in 1903 and 1928, underglaze decorated. Still in production.*

Author's Acknowledgements

IN writing this book I have relied heavily on the resources of the Royal Copenhagen Porcelain Company in Denmark and of its subsidiary in England. Although in no way sponsored by that company, or indeed approved by it, my work could not have been attempted without its generous help. In particular I must thank the current managing director Mr J. Fog-Petersen, who has given much of his valuable time to my persistent demands, and the factory's distinguished historian Mr Bredo L. Grandjean. The latter's own writings are indispensable to an understanding of the factory's past and the provenance of its wares, and I have dipped into them freely. I would also like to express particular gratitude to the keeper of the Ceramics Department of the Victoria and Albert Museum, Mr. J. V. G. Mallet, and his staff on whose expert help I, like many other writers and researchers, rely for opinion which approaches omniscience and for direction which is unfaltering.

Most of the contemporary writers on whom I have relied are acknowledged *in situ*, but I would like to thank especially Merete Bodelsen and Bevis Hillier for allowing me to make extravagant use of their works, and the editor of the Danish journal *Tidsskrift for Kunstindustri*, from which I have quoted extensively. Last but by no means least, I thank my friend of many years, Mr Harry Adler-Jensen, whose stewardship of the London-based Royal Copenhagen Company has long enlivened the British ceramics scene and whose generous friendship I have shared with many fellow countrymen in his adoptive land. Pictures are acknowledged in their place, but I must thank the office of the Lord Chamberlain for permission to use a photograph of the Flora Danica service presented to Queen Alexandra on her marriage to King Edward VII, now part of the collection of Her Majesty Queen Elizabeth at Windsor Castle; the keeper of the Danish Royal Archive at Rosenborg Palace; again, the Victoria and Albert Museum; and Mr Birger Nordlunde who supplied information and many illustrations from the factory archives.

Acknowledgements
All the pictures shown in this book are reproduced from its archives by kind permission of the Royal Copenhagen Manufactory, except those shown below (the numbers given here refer to illustration numbers, not page numbers):

British Museum, 56; Dansk Folke Museum, 24, 25; Her Majesty Queen Elizabeth II, 32; Kunstindustrimuseum, 1, 26, 49, 72, 74, 79, 86; National Museum, Stockholm, 4; Private collection, 46, 87; Rosenborg Palace Collection, 16, 17, 19, 21, 22, 23, 30, 54; Royal Copenhagen Museum, 11, 12, 13, 14, 27, 28, 37, 40, 41, 45, 47, 48, 50, 51, 57, 59, 60, 61, 62, 64, 65, 66, 67, 68, 75, 85, 89; Victoria & Albert Museum, 2, 6, 7, 8, 9, 10, 18, 69, 80, 81, 82, 83, 84, 101, 119, 157.

Contents

8 List of Illustrations

10 Introduction

CHAPTER ONE
12 A Royal Heritage

CHAPTER TWO
16 The True Porcelain

CHAPTER THREE
30 The Royal Vases

CHAPTER FOUR
42 Early On-glaze Enamelled Wares

CHAPTER FIVE
44 Flora Danica

CHAPTER SIX
56 Blue and White

CHAPTER SEVEN
72 Figures

CHAPTER EIGHT
84 Interregnum

CHAPTER NINE
86 Revival

CHAPTER TEN
96 Crystal Glazes, Stoneware and Art Faience

CHAPTER ELEVEN
114 The Modern Factory

APPENDIX A
148 The Artists and their Marks

APPENDIX B
152 The Clays

APPENDIX C
154 The Factory Marks

155 Select Bibliography

157 Index

Illustrations within text

A Royal Heritage (pages 12-16)
1 Marieberg enamel-decorated plate (1774). *Victoria and Albert Museum, London*
2 Jug and cover, Fournier period (1760-65). *Victoria and Albert Museum, London*
3 The Kobmagergade factory. From contemporary engraving

The True Porcelain (pages 16-29)
4 Frantz Henrich Mueller on porcelain coffee-cup. *National Museum, Stockholm*
5-5a Factory mark and legend
6 Porcelain bowl, c. 1775-90. *Victoria and Albert Museum, London*
7 Porcelain dish, c. 1775-90. *Victoria and Albert Museum, London*
8 Porcelain chocolate pot and cover, c. 1789. *Victoria and Albert Museum, London*
9 Porcelain tureen and cover, c. 1780. *Victoria and Albert Museum, London*
10 Porcelain cup, cover and stand, c. 1780-90. *Victoria and Albert Museum, London*
11 Vase with lid, c. 1780-85. *Royal Copenhagen Museum*
12 Battle of Copenhagen bowl, 1801-07. *Royal Copenhagen Museum*
13 Battle of Copenhagen bowl, 1801-07. *Royal Copenhagen Museum*
14 Royal Copenhagen bicentenary bowl, 1975.
15 American War of Independence bowl, 1976.

The Royal Vases (pages 30-41)
16 *Pot-pourri* vase, decorated by Ondrup, 1780. *Rosenborg Palace Collection, Copenhagen*
17 Vase decorated by Camradt, after Clemens, 1784. *Rosenborg Palace Collection, Copenhagen*
18 Vase, inferior copy of Camradt version (fig. 17). *Victoria and Albert Museum, London*
19 Vase modelled from etchings by Saly, 1788. *Rosenborg Palace Collection, Copenhagen*
20-20a Etchings for vase by J.-F.-J. Saly.
21 Vase copied from Fürstenberg model, probably by Luplau, 1789. *Rosenborg Palace Collection, Copenhagen*
22 Vase with *Fama* figures, 1789. *Rosenborg Palace Collection, Copenhagen*
23 Vase, one of pair, with wedding of Amor and Psyche. *Rosenborg Palace Collection, Copenhagen*

Early On-glaze Enamelled Wares (pages 42-43)
24 Octagonal dish, c. 1780-90. *Dansk Folke Museum, Copenhagen*
25 Sucrier and cover, c. 1780-90. *Dansk Folke Museum, Copenhagen*
26 Saucer, c. 1780-90. *Kunstindustrimuseum, Copenhagen*
27-27a Snuff-box, decorated by C. D. Luplau, c. 1777. *Royal Copenhagen Museum*

Flora Danica (pages 44-55)
28 Plate from original service. *Royal Copenhagen Museum*

29 Johann Christoph Bayer. Contemporary engraving
30 Fish-strainer from original service. *Rosenborg Palace Collection, Copenhagen*
31 Menu for Palace banquet
32 Pieces from Queen Alexandra service, now at Windsor Castle. *By gracious permission of HM the Queen, copyright reserved*
33 Tureen and cover, twentieth century
34 Ice-bell, present-day production
35 Tureen, present-day production
36 Plate, cup and saucer, and serving dish. Present-day production

Blue and White (pages 56-71)
37 Blue Flowers and Blue-Fluted, c. 1780. *Royal Copenhagen Museum*
38-39 Half and full-lace versions of Blue-Fluted pattern revived by Krog, 1885-1895. Present-day production
40 Dish, Blue-Fluted pattern, c. 1785. *Royal Copenhagen Museum*
41 Tray by Arnold Krog, 1887. *Royal Copenhagen Museum*
42 Candelabrum by Krog, 1885
43 Nineteenth-century pieces from Blue-Fluted range
44 Full-lace service designed by Krog, 1885-95
45 Early blue-painted ink-stand, c. 1775-79. *Royal Copenhagen Museum*
46 Water bottle with girdle, Blue-Flower decoration, c. 1775-79. *Private collection*
47 Pair of custard cups with Blue Flowers, c. 1780. *Royal Copenhagen Museum*
48 Oval tureen with Blue Flowers, c. 1790. *Royal Copenhagen Museum*
49 Tea caddy with Blue Flowers, probably by Hetsch, c. 1830. *Kunstindustrimuseum, Copenhagen*
50 Tureen with Blue Flowers, c. 1820-25. *Royal Copenhagen Museum*
51 Oval tureen in rococo style, 1841. *Royal Copenhagen Museum*
52 Curved shape with Blue Flowers, by Krog c. 1903
53 Present-day Blue Flower plate

Figures (pages 72-83)
54 Bust of Queen Juliane Marie by A. C. Luplau, 1781. *Rosenborg Palace Collection, Copenhagen*
55 Europa by Luplau, c. 1780. Modern copy
55a Detail from Europa figure
56 Lunéville figure, Shepherd with Kid, by P.-L. Cyfflé. *British Museum, London*
57 Copenhagen Shepherd with Kid, c. 1781. *Royal Copenhagen Museum*
58 Modern copy of another Copenhagen version of Shepherd with Kid
59 The Patriot, c. 1780. *Royal Copenhagen Museum*
60 Bathing Venus, c. 1780. *Royal Copenhagen Museum*
61 Naval Officer and Drummer, c. 1792. *Royal Copenhagen Museum*
62 Peddling Woman with Hen and Eggs, c. 1780. *Royal Copenhagen Museum*

63 Lady and Gentleman Dancing, c. 1790. Modern copy
64 Bacchus on Rock, by A. C. Luplau, c. 1780. *Royal Copenhagen Museum*
65 Elephant and Lady or 'Patience', c. 1783. *Royal Copenhagen Museum*
66 Shepherd Group, c. 1780. *Royal Copenhagen Museum*
67 Miners' Group, c. 1780. *Royal Copenhagen Museum*
68 Peasant Woman (from Norwegian series) 1783-1811. *Royal Copenhagen Museum*

Interregnum (pages 84-85)
69-69a Hebe after Thorvaldsen. *Victoria and Albert Museum, London*

Revival (pages 86-95)
70 Portrait: Arnold Krog, Art Director 1885-1916. *Factory archive*
71 Krog drawing for 'Immortelle' revival, 1885. *Factory archive*
72 Vase with Mouse by Krog, 1887. *Kunstindustrimuseum, Copenhagen*
73 Illustration from Japanese guide, c. 1850. *Factory archive*
74 Dish by Krog, 1887. *Kunstindustrimuseum, Copenhagen*
75 Dish by Krog, 1886. *Royal Copenhagen Museum*
76 Mocha pot, cup and saucer by Krog, 1897.
77 Mocha pot, sugar bowl, cup and saucer by Krog, 1909.

Crystal Glazes, Stoneware and Art Faience (pages 96-113)
78 The Potter by Jais Nielsen
79 Vase with *oeil de chat* glaze by Engelhardt, 1897. *Kunstindustrimuseum, Copenhagen*
80 Porcelain vase with green glaze by Engelhardt, 1899. *Victoria and Albert Museum, London*
81 Sèvres *porcelain nouvelle* vase with turquoise glaze, 1880. *Victoria and Albert Museum, London*
82 Vase by Chaplet with crimson glaze, c. 1900. *Victoria and Albert Museum, London*
83 Crystal-glazed vase by Engelhardt, 1897. *Victoria and Albert Museum, London*
84 Copenhagen crystal-glaze vase, c. 1900. *Victoria and Albert Museum, London*
85 Vases with crystal glazes, 1900-1910. *Royal Copenhagen Museum*
86 Stoneware jar by Nordström, *Kunstindustrimuseum, Copenhagen*
87 Stoneware jar by Nordström. *Private collection*
88 Stoneware jar by Axel Salto. *Royal Copenhagen Museum*
89 Stoneware bottle by Nordström. *Royal Copenhagen Museum*
90 Stoneware figure group by Knud Kyhn, c. 1920
91 Stoneware Hippopotamus by Knud Kyhn, 1928
92 Pontius Pilate. Stoneware group by Jais Nielsen, 1927
93 Stoneware vase by Axel Salto, 1943
94 Stoneware vases by Nils Thorsson, 1970s
95 Art Faience by Christian Joachim, 1903

The Modern Factory (pages 114-135)
96 Stoneware by Bente Hansen, 1980
97 The Princess on the Pea, figure by Gerhard Henning, 1911
98 National Costume Figures from Amager by Carl Martin-Hansen, 1906
99 Moongirl, figure by Gerhard Henning, 1924
100 Icelandic Girl, figure by Arno Malinowsky, c. 1931. *Victoria and Albert Museum, London*
101 Weeping Faun, figure by Gerhard Henning, 1910
102 Three figures by Malinowsky, 1924-26
103-103a Chessmen by Siegfried Wagner, 1913
104 The Rock and the Wave, figure group by Th. Lundberg, 1899
105 Elephant and Deer by Knud Kyhn, stoneware, 1957
106 Vase by Mogens Andersen, stoneware, 1973
107 Stoneware by Snorre Stephensen, 1979
108 Stoneware by Ivan Weiss, 1974
109 Stoneware bowl by Axel Salto, 1949
110 Flask and vase by Nils Thorsson, 1958/6
111-113 Stoneware by Bente Hansen, 1981-82
114 Diana stoneware range by Nils Thorsson
115-118 Modern tableware

Commemorative and Annual Wares (pages 136-147)
119 Porcelain plate to mark coronation of Edward VII, 1902, *Victoria and Albert Museum, London*
120 'Portraits of Old Copenhagen' series, from 1978
121-124 Historical Plates, from 1975
125-127 Year Mugs, from 1967
128 The Artist's Egg by Robert Jacobsen, from 1975
129-132 Mothers' Day Plates, from 1971
133-150 Christmas Plates

151-155 Porcelain figures by Christian Thomsen, 1898-1921
151 Princess and Swineherd
152 Peasant Women Gossiping
153 Boy with Calf
154 Girl with Calf
155 Goose Girl

156 Blue Fish *(Coelacanth)* earthenware by Jeanne Grut, 1963
157 Fox Barking, porcelain, by Erik Nielsen, 1910. *Victoria and Albert Museum, London*
158 Mouse on Cheese, porcelain, by Erik Nielsen, 1912
159 Barn Owls, porcelain, by Arnold Krog, 1901
160 Amherst Pheasants, by Andrea Nielsen, 1907-17
161 Snowy Owl and Long-eared Owl by Peter Herold, 1917/1912
162 Kingfishers by Peter Herold, 1915-22

Introduction

WHEN the first English account of the history of Royal Copenhagen Porcelain appeared in 1918, from the pen of that chatty chronicler of the world's potteries Arthur Hayden, the press received it with an enthusiasm usually reserved for the more successful theatrical first nights.

The Times, observing that the famous Danish manufactory had by then been in existence for almost 150 years without adequate recognition in an English history, described the publication of Hayden's book as 'a tardy act of reparation' for damage inflicted on the factory by British guns in 1807. Hitherto, the only guides to the Copenhagen wares had been an article written by Hayden in the *Artist* magazine in 1902, which was subsequently reprinted and sold in second-hand bookshops at the enormous price of five shillings, and a pictorial extravaganza by the same author issued in 1911. M. Louis Solon, the distinguished ceramic artist of Sèvres and Minton, on seeing a copy of the former publication, commented: 'It looks as though, in its course from East to West, ceramic painting has deserted its old home to take refuge in the North. *C'est du Nord aujourd'hui que nous vient la lumière!*'

The decision to publish a new and up-to-date history in 1983 might be seen as another belated act of reparation. The need is apparent. Hayden's book has long been out of print, and it has fallen out of favour in modern times, largely because of its uncritical view of the Copenhagen masters and their works. In any case it is out of date, recent research by the factory's resident curator and other historians having shown much of the accepted testimony, whether in Danish, German, French or English accounts, to be questionable and often misleading.

Some explanation is nevertheless required for the appearance of this work, and for its authorship.

It is the realisation of a long-held aim, which has been denied by contrary loyalties and by the demands of writing in a quite separate field. For some twenty years I was engaged as a writer and press adviser in promoting English pottery, a subject to which I remain attached by that strange mystique known only to those who deal in the potters' arts, which is compounded of admiration of skills beyond one's own reach, a sense of history and a dash of patriotism. In more recent years I have edited pottery journals in tandem with a literary life which has involved me in the history and exploration of the Arab countries of the Middle East. The two interests have always had a bearing on each other.

Any devotion to the crafts must inevitably turn eastward in the search for origin and inspiration. My own interest early on was captured not only by China, the source of all ceramic invention, but by the archaeological finds in ancient Sumeria, Babylonia and Assyria, and by the later tin-glazed wares of Mesopotamia which found their way westward *via* the Mediterranean, where they took on the name *maiolica*, and then northward where they acquired the generic name *delft*.

But in a working life which happily combined sympathetic interests in English ceramics and Arab history, I retained a devout and sometimes secretive allegiance to the European factory which I believed to be all-in-all the finest of the western custodians of the potter's art, Royal Copenhagen.

No other European porcelain house has survived for so long and yet maintained so urbane an artistic tradition. Other factories can claim priority in time and in the production of certain patterns and decorations. None has endured so vigorously, working with sustained distinction in all the chief ceramic bodies, earthenware, porcelain and stoneware; and claiming age by age a place in the vanguard of decorative art.

Some of the finest achievements of the Danish royal factory have been in fields which have offered negligible commercial reward: in stonewares, for example, which most other large manufactories are content to leave to the studio potter and the small craft concern. Some factories have sought to survive on the strength of tradition, perpetuating the wares of the eighteenth century with ever diminishing conviction and skill, reproducing old hand decorations by lithographic transfer while making loud protestations of manifest artistry. Royal Copenhagen has absorbed its own tradition with pride, but it has never used the past as an excuse for mediocrity in the present. It has absorbed and adapted the works of other factories and other cultures – plagiarism being the accepted cornerstone of ceramic art – but it has always infused such works with its own identifiable style and its own high standards. In short, its distinguishing quality has nearly always been contemporary excellence. If, in the present, Royal Copenhagen is renowned for three of the most beautiful and persistent patterns in the entire history of European porcelain manufacture – the famous Immortelle decorated services, Blue Flowers which derive from the *Deutsche Blumen* of the eighteenth century, and its own Flora Danica – it yet stands head and shoulders above all others as the protagonist of good modern design in ceramics. Therein lies the source of my own enthusiasm.

The Flute Player. On-glaze decorated, first made c. 1780. Artist unknown. Illustration and detail from modern copy.

A Royal Heritage

[1] Grandjean, Bredo L., *The Royal Copenhagen Porcelain Manufactory, 1775-1975*, Copenhagen, 1975, p.9.

[2] Phillips, John Goldsmith, *China Trade Porcelain*, USA, 1956; Grandjean, Bredo L., *Dansk ostindisk porcelaen importen fra Kanton, c.1700-1822*, Copenhagen, 1965.

[3] Yule, Sir Henry, *Marco Polo*, Murray, 1921. See also Hillier, Bevis, *Pottery and Porcelain 1700-1914*, Weidenfeld, 1968, p.90, 'pourcelaine'.

THE Royal Copenhagen Porcelain Manufactory came into being officially on 1 May 1775[1] when a meeting was held at the Danish capital in response to the 'most gracious wish' of Her Majesty Queen Juliane Marie. It was decided that three wavy lines should be the mark of the company.

But the story of porcelain manufacture in Denmark and the true provenance of the royal factory pre-date that meeting by some fifteen years in their complex, interwoven origins.

In England the term 'Royal', so often used in connection with the great china factories of the kingdom, implies patronage. In Continental Europe it has always designated ownership. No British monarch has ever owned a china factory, or indeed any other commercial undertaking. On the Continent such ownership has been absolute, the mark of regal prowess, of kingly enterprise and artistic discrimination; a cut on the court escutcheon to be prized and honoured alongside victory on the battlefield and the nationally advantageous marriage dowry.

As in most things artistic, western endeavour found its earliest inspiration in the east. When the brothers Nicolo and Maffeo Polo returned to Venice from Central Asia in 1268 they carried with them rich gifts and a golden tablet addressed to the Pope from the Great Khan, Kublai, who conquered China and, eleven years after the return of the Polos, instituted the Moghul Yüan dynasty. In 1270 the brothers set out on a second journey, accompanied by Nicolo's son Marco, to make the first recorded trek along the silk road from the Mediterranean to China, returning with more gifts: jewels, fabrics, metalwork and examples of the potter's craft which were to inflame Europe with envy and ambition. By the turn of the thirteenth century the nations and city states of Europe were engaged in a race to accumulate the riches of the East, and to emulate eastern crafts.

A century later the ships of the maritime nations opened up the sea route to China, bringing home with them increasing quantities of dishes with which to grace the noble tables of the west: wares decorated in unimagined hues on a body of gleaming white, jewel-like in the transmission of light through body, glaze and decorated surface. By the sixteenth century, with the formation of the first Indies Companies, the trade in Chinese 'export' wares had become enormous. The finest articles from the kilns of Ching-tê-chên and other centres of pottery making, the Imperial wares, were reserved for the royal households of China, the Ming emperors; of the rest, much was heaped into the holds of the Indies ships, serving as ballast as well as a highly prized commodity.[2]

Europe, lacking a name for the Oriental pottery it craved, set out on an ingenious etymological excursion. The Venetians, who opened up both land and sea routes to China, had a special liking for the so-called 'eggshell' wares and they compared them with the cowrie shell of a common sea creature known colloquially as *porcella*, diminutive of *porco* (pig), from the arched shape of its back. Thus *pocellana*, and the French *porcelaine*. The word must have been in use before the end of the thirteenth century since Marco Polo used it to describe the delicate wares he had been shown on his visit to Fukien Province prior to the year 1290.[3]

The English-speaking peoples, not to be persuaded by so romantic a notion, looked to the country of origin and called the sought-after wares of the East 'china'.

The names given by Europeans to the Chinese potters' wares have presented problems of definition and aesthetic understanding ever since. In compartmentalising the works of craftsmen and artists whose essential characteristic was a painstaking, disciplined and sympathetic devotion to clays and earths in all their varied and contrasting forms, in making comparative assessments of value and worth (usually to the detriment of one ceramic composition as against another), western potters have done themselves a great disservice.

The Chinese used only the word *Yao*,

which has roughly the meaning of 'ware', with respect to every pottery article, usually attached to the name of the district in which it was made. They did not distinguish between one composition and another, recognising only the essential compatability between a given body – be it of the coarsest earth or the purest white clay – and the glazes and colours which would produce the desired result in terms of appearance and utility.

Such contrasting attitudes have a profound relevance to the history of the Royal Copenhagen Manufactory. Although the Danes necessarily embraced the nomenclature of the West, they were never imprisoned by it. Two centuries after the official foundation of the company, an English historian of the decorative arts, looking back at one of its most creative periods, observed:

> Royal Copenhagen was the least reactionary of the great European factories.[4]

The statement loses none of its significance for its negative praise. It would have been as true to say that it was the 'most progressive', but no more or less illustrative of the fact that the potters and ceramic artists of Copenhagen have always resisted the temptation to engage in artificial value judgements, to raise one ceramic composition above another. They have never made the spurious claim that one clay body or glaze or decorative technique is necessarily superior to others. At the present, as generally in the past, they work in an intellectual mainstream which derives in a basic sense from that philosophy which first raised the skills of anonymous potters to the level of the highest art: keeping open a window on the world at large, taking note of trends in art, fashion and design, and above all instilling in their work that veneration of material and devotion to craft which were the alpha and omega of Chinese achievement.

Imitation is seldom as simple a matter as its detractors imagine. It took Europe the best part of half a millennium from its first sight of the Oriental wares to the conjuring of a likeness. In the meantime, alchemists, silversmiths and potters at the courts of Florence and France found costly substitutes for the clays that formed the foundation of Chinese porcelain. They devised artificial compounds of earthen clays, glass frits, soapstone, bone ash and other substances, which fused into a vitreous entity at the relatively low temperature of the earthenware bisque kiln. They coated the resultant fired body with a lead glaze. From its tendency to collapse in the kiln, this expedient but often beautiful substitute for the real thing was called *pâte tendre*, or soft paste.

In spite of all its inherent disadvantages, the potters of Medici Florence and St Cloud and Vincennes in France worked wonders with this surrogate material, though they had to accept the commercial penalty – as did their successors in Britain, Denmark and other places of manufacture – of enormous losses and gross deformities in firing. The soft paste was to survive for two centuries, competing with the fine white and cream glazed earthenwares of the time and reaching an artistic zenith in the works of the French factory at Vincennes, later Sèvres. Even after the discovery of the secret of true porcelain in the first decade of the eighteenth century, manufacture in the artificial body went on creditably, if unprofitably, in France, England, Denmark and elsewhere.[5]

'True' hard-paste porcelain is said to have been discovered in Europe in the year 1709 when Johann Friedrich Boettger, goldsmith and alchemist to the court of August II, Elector of Saxony and King of Poland (August the Strong), produced a white ware[6] composed chiefly of a fine infusible clay known to the Chinese as *kaolin* and a felspathic stone which Chinese potters called *petuntse*, literally 'white bricks'. Boettger obtained his clays from deposits at the nearby region of Aue. Thus was the mystery unravelled, a mystery to which the Chinese had clung for some 1,500 years.

Boettger's work represented a landmark in the history of European pottery manufacture. Yet it was, in its nomenclature at least, equivocal. In the previous year, 1708, Boettger had announced the 'discovery' of porcelain when he produced a hard, impervious redware. And in the previous century the English potter John Dwight of Fulham had not only produced redwares which were described and sold as 'porcelaine'; he had been granted letters patent in 1684 asserting his exclusive right to make 'opacous red and dark coloured porcelaine and china'. Nine years later he was given leave by the English law courts to take action against several alleged imitators, including the Dutch immigrants John and David Elers and three members of the Wedgwood family, to restrain them from infringing his patent.[7]

It is clear from the acrimonious proceedings that followed Dwight's litigation that to potters of the time, and indeed to the law as it

[4] Hillier, Bevis, *Pottery and Porcelain, 1700-1914*, (Social History of the Decorative Arts Series), London, 1968, p.335.

[5] Florentine (Medici) wares 1568-87; St Cloud c. 1695-1773; Vincennes 1740; Sèvres from 1756. See Honey, W. B., *French Porcelain*, Faber, 1950.

[6] Meissen and the European discovery. See Honey, W. B., *Dresden China*, London, 1934; Monkhouse, Cosmo, *Chinese Porcelain*, London, 1901; Savage, George, *Porcelain through the Ages*, London, 1961.

[7] Dwight and the Elers brothers. See Shaw, S., *History of the Staffordshire Potteries*; Burton, Wm, *History and Description of English Earthenware*; Wedgwood, Josiah C., *Staffordshire Pottery and its History*, p.27ff 'Elers and Art' with summary of law suits 1693-94. *Memoirs of George Elers, 1777-1842*, ed. Monson and Leveson-Gower. Redware at Fulham and Staffordshire, and Elers' artistry, see Dr Martin Lister in *Philosophical Transactions*, vol.xvii, 1693.

ROYAL COPENHAGEN

[8] Bornholm kaolin deposits discovered 1755. Another unconnected factory est. Marieberg island 1758. Wares marked 'MB' with three crowns superior. Earthenware produced from 1758 to 1766. Soft paste in French style under direction of Pierre Bethevin of Mennecy 1766-69. From 1770 to 1788 a hybrid paste, often with tin glaze.

1 *Marieberg enamel-decorated plate. Mark three crowns over line, MB in monogram, and painter's mark AF. 1774. Probably hybrid paste (felspar-enriched earthenware). Diameter 10⅛in (258mm). Victoria and Albert Museum, London.*

[9] Johann Gottlieb Mehlhorn from Meissen to Copenhagen 1754. Returned 1762. Brother of Meissen painter Johann Gottfried Mehlhorn. Johann Christian Ludwig von Luecke, Modelmeister Meissen 1728, sculptor to Saxon Court 1739-50, Vienna 1750, Copenhagen 1752-54.

[10] Hillier, *op.cit.*, 'Social Status', p.39.

[11] Fournier, see Hayden, Arthur, *Chats on Royal Copenhagen Porcelain*, Fisher Unwin, 1918.

[12] Hayden, *op.cit.*

stood in England, the word 'porcelain' was associated with the susceptibility of a clay to the intense heat of the *grand feu*, and with the homogeneity of the resultant body. It had little or nothing to do with whiteness, translucency or the employment of any particular ceramic ingredients.

Be that as it may, Boettger's hard-paste white ware, actual production of which began at the Meissen factory near Dresden in 1710, marked the onset of 'true' porcelain manufacture in Europe, and a revolution in the potter's craft.

2 *Jug and cover. Copenhagen soft-paste porcelain, Fournier period, decorated with on-glaze enamels and gilt. Mark 'F5', 1760-65. Height with cover 5½in (140mm). Victoria and Albert Museum, London. Similar jug in Copenhagen Kunstindustrimuseum, probably painted by Georg Richter.*

The first porcelain made in Denmark[8] was of the capricious soft-paste body. A factory was established in 1755, at the behest of King Frederik V, near the famous Blue Tower, but there is evidence of experimental work even before that date under the guidance of the Saxon potters Johann Gottlieb Mehlhorn and Johann von Luecke.[9] The former had been seduced from the Meissen factory during a period of dissension between painters and other craftsmen over pay differentials.[10] The latter came from Vienna. Both were craftsmen of considerable ability and experience but there is little evidence of fruitful work during their residence in Copenhagen. Perhaps the paucity of actual achievement was the consequence of unsuccessful attempts to master the use of the hard paste, for it was certainly the intention of Frederik V that the Danish factory should emulate the works of Meissen, Vienna, Berlin and the other royal factories of Europe which had been established after the death of Boettger in 1719.

Another imported talent in the early days of the soft-paste factory was that of the Englishman (or perhaps Scotsman) Denis McCarthy, who was called from London to the Danish capital in April 1753. He remained for less than a year and disappeared into oblivion, but one item is preserved in the museum of Rosenborg Palace as testimony to his presence: a signed relief portrait of Frederik V.

It was not until 1760 that the Blue Tower establishment can be said to have entered upon a productive phase. In that year the Frenchman Louis Fournier[11] became its manager and during the six years of his stewardship the factory was modestly successful in the production of soft-paste wares derivative of Sèvres, the royal French factory, in design and decoration.

The influence of Sèvres modelling and decoration on Fournier and his artist assistants such as the Danish sculptor Johannes Wiedewelt is hardly surprising. It was the climactic era of the royal French factory and the Sèvres reputation was pervasive. It is recorded that in 1758 Louis XV of France had sent Frederik of Denmark a fine service in the *pâte tendre* with a green ground, decorated with figures, flowers and birds.[12] The inventory of the time shows it to have been valued at 30,000 livres. It must have provided Fournier's artists with an admirable model for their soft-paste wares, and the surviving pieces suggest a close though not slavish adherence to the Sèvres patterns. The Copenhagen articles are lacking in the supreme confidence shown by the French in the application of their on-glaze enamels, with their uninhibited use of rich and sometimes flamboyant colours on birds and flowers, for example. All the same, they are sensitive and skilled examples of decoration and firing in one of the most difficult and unpredictable of all ceramic mediums.

That the products of Fournier's factory posed no serious challenge to the trade and reputation of the royal establishment at Sèvres, where the French director of the Copenhagen factory had worked as sculptor and modeller,[13] is attested by the French ambassador to the Danish capital, Jean-François Ogier. On 7 June 1763 he allayed the suspicions of Louis XV with the words:

> Cette manufacture établie depuis deux ans, si on peut donner ce nom a l'établissement qui a été fait, n'est encore composé que du chef de cette entreprise, qui prepare les matières et qui dirige les fours, et de deux tourneurs ou sculpteurs, et n'a encore produit que quelque douzaines d'assiettes, de compotiers, de moutardiers, sucriers, et autres petits vases. . . . Une pareil établissement pourra difficilement faire un objet de commerce et n'a été jusqu'à present que celuy d'un amusement que Mons. Cte de Moltke a essayé de prouver au Roy son maître.

An 'amusement of the Prince' it would chiefly remain until Fournier returned to France, but not an altogether unhappy epitaph to Moltke's faith and support.

The factory mark was a cursive letter F and the figure 5, representing Frederik V and not, as is sometimes thought, Fournier. It has been suggested that the work of the soft-paste establishment was influenced by Fürstenberg, as well as by the pervasive modelling and decorative styles of Sèvres. There has even been conjecture that some pieces made at Copenhagen in the brief period 1760-66 may have been wrongly attributed to the German factory.[14] The evidence is slim, however. Admittedly Charles I, Duke of Brunswick and the owner of the Schloss Fürstenberg factory, was the brother of Queen Juliane Marie, and it is not without significance that the director of Fürstenberg, J. G. von Langen, left the service of the Duke in 1763 to take up an appointment in Denmark. But the real significance of that connection was to be felt later on when another factory was founded on the basis of the 'true' porcelain body. In any case, it would not be difficult to distinguish the hard-paste wares of Fürstenberg from the Copenhagen soft paste.

During the first three years of the factory by the Blue Tower, the Seven Years' War was raging. By the time that struggle reached its conclusion in 1763 the balance of power had changed in Europe, and in the world at large. So, too, had the structure of the European porcelain industry changed. Frederick the Great of Prussia had annexed Silesia, occupied Dresden and removed to Berlin many of the records and leading workmen of the Meissen establishment. Britain had added Canada and India to its dominions. For many European countries the outlook was bleak. For Britain, its navy in control of the oceans, a golden age beckoned in which its potters would share, though they rejected from the outset the Continental preoccupation with true porcelain and, with the exception of a few short-lived ventures, retained in perpetuity the existing earthenware technology.

In 1766 Frederik V of Denmark died and the 17-year-old manikin King Christian VII came to the throne. Fournier went home to France and the porcelain factory by the Blue Tower fell into disuse. Denmark, like most of the European countries, suffered great privation in its everyday life, and its suffering was made none the more bearable by the excesses of the new court. But it was an age of popular distress and royal abandon. Kaendler, the great modelmeister of Meissen, had reflected the courtly spirit of the age in his later figures which seemed to anticipate Mozart (who was ten years old in 1766 and already famous), dancing the minuet on the shelves of the rich. Bustelli, the genius of the porcelain figure, had joined the Nymphenburg factory in 1754. The Copenhagen factory was about to find a new lease of life at the tail-end of the era of masked balls and junketings, of frivolity and flippancy; the age of the arabesque and the 'frothy petticoat'.[15]

[13] Fournier worked at both Vincennes and Chantilly, and returned to the former when it was moved to Sèvres.

[14] Hayden, *op.cit.* p.36.

[15] Hillier, *op.cit.*

Altogether 171 pieces from the Fournier period are known to have survived to the present day. No contemporary list of the soft-paste production exists but it is unlikely to have exceeded a few hundred pieces. *Factory archives*, note to author July 1974.

2
The True Porcelain

3 The royal factory façade at Kobmagergade, from a contemporary engraving.

AS we have seen, the era of true porcelain manufacture was inaugurated in Denmark in 1775 and ascribed by history to the initiative of the Dowager Queen Juliane Marie. But it was the persistence and untiring work of a Copenhagen apothecary that made possible the establishment of a new factory in the Kobmagergade[16] capable of producing high-fired wares with those qualities of stability in the kiln, durability in use and delicacy in appearance which are the marks of hard-paste porcelain.

Frantz Henrich Mueller was born at Copenhagen on 17 November 1732. From the age of 15 he was apprenticed to a pharmacist and became a keen student of the natural sciences. At the early age of 27 he was appointed supervisor of the Mint at the Bank of Copenhagen. It was during the latter appointment that he began to contemplate, and seek

[16] Built in 1765.

THE TRUE PORCELAIN

support for, a Danish porcelain factory, in succession to the old soft-paste factory. In 1765, the year before the closure of the Blue Tower establishment, he began to look for financial support, and to plan a secret if largely fruitless tour of the great continental centres of porcelain making – Fürstenburg, Meissen and Berlin. His application to take over the workshop of the soft-paste manufactory had been submitted jointly with Johann Georg Richter, an artist who had worked at the Blue Tower from its experimental period which began in 1752. Although that application was granted, the King was unwilling to support a new venture. He had burnt his fingers in supporting Fournier's 'excessively expensive' attempts at porcelain making.

With the fun-loving old monarch Frederik V went the statesman and art patron who had been his Prime Minister, Count Moltke. A new regime of ministers and hangers-on surrounded the young Christian VII. Despite the lack of royal support, however, and in the face of a deplorable deterioration in the nation's finances, Mueller continued his experiments with the clays that had been discovered in the early days of the soft-paste factory. If his first prospectus had resulted in the sale of only one share, he was at least able by 1773 to present the new sovereign with his first few pieces of 'hard-fired transparent porcelain', and to announce the acquisition of premises suitable for a factory in the Kobmagergade. Christian VII expressed 'no objections' to his plans. But

4 *Frantz Henrich Mueller in his laboratory, illustrated on a coffee-cup with floral wreath in gold and blue border, bearing an inscription in gold:*
  The finest senses may well pleased be –
  When Nature leans on Science for her aid –
  But art is wedlock with Utility –
  Demands from skill a double debt be paid.
National Museum, Stockholm.

power now resided with the Dowager Queen, Juliane Marie.

In 1774 Mueller presented to her his plan for a Danish Porcelain Manufactory, as is attested by the factory's Protocol No.1, covering the period 1775-79:

> When HER MAJESTY QUEEN JULIANE MARIE in the year 1774 graciously received from Frantz Henrich Mueller, apothecary, an invitation to participate in a Danish porcelain factory, Her Majesty expressed regret that the plan apparently had not met with approval. . . .[17]

The prodigious efforts of the brilliant and tireless apothecary were pursued against a background not only of commercial indifference but also of great national stress in which the virtual disintegration of the Court was both symptom and cause. In the tangle of royal alliances that brought the nations of the Continent into uneasy connection with the throne of Great Britain, Christian VII had married the 15-year-old Caroline Matilde, sister of George III. The young couple were bedevilled by court intrigue in which Madame de Plessen, Queen Caroline Matilde's lady-in-waiting, and the royal physician John Frederick Struensee played consummate parts. Subsequent events in which the painted men and women of a dissolute court played out a drama which was to lead to the imprisonment and exile of the young 'Queen of Tears' and the beheading of Struensee and his partner in crime Brandt, constitute a bitter and colourful episode in the history of Denmark; and they nearly precipitated a war between Britain and Denmark.[18]

The Dowager Queen, accompanied by her son Frederik the Heir Presumptive and a gang of conspirators, used the occasion of a masked ball at the royal palace on 16 January 1772 to seize the young Queen, together with Struensee and Brandt, and to impose exile and divorce on the much abused Matilde. The absolute rule of the malevolent – yet in many ways wise – old Queen was thereby established. At her side was her own son Frederik, half-brother of the King, as heir presumptive. The infant Crown Prince Frederik, her grandson, remained in the shadow of his gibbering father Christian VII, the royal cipher whose future role was to append his name to documents of state. And it was Juliane Marie who, through her secretary Theodor Holm, made known 'her gracious wish that this project, which to all appearances seemed to be a useful one, should be put into effect'.

Thus the Dowager Queen lent her decisive support to Mueller's plans[19] and brought about the realisation of his dream. At the meeting of 1 May 1775, when the Queen's proposal for a factory mark of three wavy lines was adopted, Holm the royal secretary was elected to the board along with Guldberg, the heir presumptive's private secretary (both men were later made peers and became known as Holmskjold and Hoegh Guldberg respectively). Among other founder directors was General Eickstedt who had been one of the conspirators at the masked ball and, in less

[17]Grandjean, *op.cit.*, p.9.

[18]Wilkins, W. H., *A Queen of Tears*, London, 1904.

[19]Grandjean, *op.cit.*, p.10.

5 and 5a *Factory mark and legend, based on the three Danish waterways, Oresund, Storebelt and Lillebelt – Sound and Great and Little Belts – recorded in opening page of factory Protocol No. 1. Here shown on reverse of blue-painted dish, c. 1785, and on base of modern cup. Mark 71:31b is the factory museum identification.*

fortunate circumstances, might have lost his head for high treason. He and Holm were major shareholders. Mueller, who had entertained thoughts of a directorship, was allowed to purchase a single share and was nominated factory manager.[20] At a prior meeting, which had taken place on 13 March 1775, the company was granted a monopoly for fifty years in the manufacture of porcelain in Denmark and its dominions.[21]

The part played by the Queen was emphasised by a Danish historian writing within two years of the factory's founding:

> The honour for bringing about this arrangement, so important to our nation, falls to our benefactress, Her Majesty Queen Juliane Marie, and to the King's brother, the heir presumptive, Prince Frederik.[22]

If a note of sycophancy is discernible, we should not judge the old Queen too harshly or necessarily detect abjectness in the protagonists of her own time.

As a distinguished historian of porcelain in the late twentieth century (and the factory's late curator) has observed:

> Many harshly critical words have been written about the Queen, and not without reason. But perhaps one cannot blame her for nurturing a desire to reign herself, having had Struensee executed thereby giving herself the opportunity. Moreover, as the bitter widow of a popular bibulous libertine, with a mentally disturbed stepson on the throne, her own weak untalented son as heir presumptive and a small boy as Crown Prince, she must also, as the only adult and experienced rational being in the family, have regarded it as her duty towards the very concept of absolutism.[23]

Nonetheless, the royal hand should not be allowed to obscure the work and enterprise of the indomitable Mueller, to whose strength of will, resilience and patience in the face of obstacles that would have daunted lesser men, Royal Copenhagen owes an overwhelming debt for its early achievements both in technique and also in artistry.

If the influence of Fürstenberg was at best conjectural during the six years' duration of the old soft-paste factory, it was conspicuous early in the period of Mueller and his royal patron. In 1776 A. C. Luplau was induced to leave the Duke of Brunswick's factory by the river Weser, where he had been employed for eighteen years, and to join the Copenhagen factory as model-master. Doubtless the appointment was made after consultation with the ex-director of Fürstenberg, J. G. von Langen,[24] but it has been suggested that in order to obtain the services of this distinguished craftsman Mueller had to pay part of the salary from his own pocket.[25] If there is any truth in that allegation, there can have been little enthusiasm among the board of directors. At about the same time five workers[26] were engaged from the Meissen factory by August Hennings the secretary of the Danish Legation at Dresden. It was clearly an underhand arrangement and in the ensuing diplomatic fuss the Saxon ambassador to Copenhagen was instructed to demand the recall of the men. Two of them were finally persuaded to return home.

In the first four years, with the aid of these experienced artists and artisans, Mueller was able to produce some on-glaze enamelled wares of high merit in modelling and painting. Some surface deformities, caused chiefly by iron impurities in the glaze, were deftly covered over by the bold application of purple, red and other oxide colours; and most contained the monograms of their recipients in gold, for they were invariably made as gifts for the royal family and its friends. The early commercial policy of the factory was not designed to encourage the more prudent investors, and in 1779 they prompted the directors to stave off bankruptcy by inviting Christian VII to become the factory's sole owner. The proposal was accepted on 21 April 1779, and the existing shares redeemed at a premium of twenty times their original value. If, as has been suggested, 'Queen Juliane Marie placed the pen in the King's hand',[27] then nobody complained.

At a meeting on 30 June of the same year the name of the company was officially changed to *Den Kongelige Danske Porcelains Fabrik*, and so it has remained for two centuries: the Royal Porcelain Manufactory. Mueller and his assistants had laid the foundation of artistic and commercial fortune in the first four or five years of hard and sometimes bitter endeavour. The factory would reap a rich harvest under its royal owner, but for the moment the situation was a businessman's nightmare. By the end of the first year of the new regime, accumulated stock amounted to more than 100,000 pieces of expensive and often elaborately decorated porcelain. In those days porcelain was sold almost exclusively through jewellers' and silversmiths' shops and, weight for weight, was valued as highly as gold. In the absence of commercial experience or organisation, it was decided that the only way to provide finance for the company was to sell its

[20] Mueller is sometimes referred to as 'Factory Inspector'. See Grandjean, *The Flora Danica Service*, Forum, Copenhagen, 1973.

[21] Hayden, *op.cit.*, p.56.

[22] Grandjean, *op.cit.*, quotes Andreas Schytte, 1777, p.10.

[23] Grandjean, *op.cit.*, p.10.

[24] Grandjean, *op.cit.*, p.11.

[25] Hayden, *op.cit.*, p.59.

[26] Hayden, *op.cit.*, p.60, says three workmen were brought from Meissen, but expelled by Mueller because 'supercilious manners (and) higher wages brought trouble in the factory'.

[27] Grandjean, *op.cit.*, p.12.

ROYAL COPENHAGEN

wares from the factory premises, and a shop was created on the second floor at Kobmagergade. The King gave permission for the sale of wares to commence on 1 March 1780. The editor of the *Copenhagen Gazette* regarded the occasion as of sufficient importance to justify a Latin verse on the front page, but even his learned panegyric failed to induce the public to climb to the second floor of the royal factory's premises. There were nine paying customers on the first day, led by the Dowager Queen's lady-in-waiting who bought two hyacinth jars. The Royal Copenhagen shop was to become an internationally renowned feature of the manufactory, an acknowledged tourist resort (though it would be forced to change its site over the years). For the time being, however, it did little to reverse the commercial trend. Sales for the rest of its initial year amounted to an average of three pieces a day.

Porcelain evolved in Europe with inspired timing. It bridged, as no other medium could, the transition from the baroque to the rococo, from the mood of heavy and sometimes ecstatic theatricality to that of the masked ball, the *commedia dell' arte*, the crinolined lady and the whispered intimacy. The baroque, the true

6 Porcelain bowl, enamel and gilt decoration, c. 1775-90. Mark and 'M + K' impressed. Wavy rim, side moulded with four rococo scroll panels, separated by wavy vertical bands. Panels painted alternately with birds and bouquets, outlined by gilt scrolls. Small insects and leaves painted to conceal flaws. Height 4½in (114mm). Diameter 9⅝in (245mm). Victoria and Albert Museum, London.

province of architect and sculptor, came late to northern Europe, stopped in its tracks by the Thirty Years' War. When it arrived it expressed overwhelmingly the dramatic visual art of the Bernini school, tempered by the so-called Fiammingo tradition of Duquesnoy.

There are no hard and fast lines of demarcation. It would be futile to try to point to a moment in time when one mood, one style gave rise to another; when one superseded the other. Indeed, there are aspects of the baroque which seem, in spirit, to span two centuries or more; to anticipate William Morris and the arts and crafts movement of the nineteenth century:

> Bernini... gave a Publique Opera... where he painted the scenes, cut the Statues, invented the Engines, composed the Musique, writ the Comedy and built the Theater all himselfe.[28]

The rococo grew out of the baroque, and found its apotheosis in the sublime invention of Mozart, the carefree subjects of Fragonard; in the *style pittoresque* and the masterly alliance of the silversmith's and potter's skills which manifested itself in the candlesticks of Juste-Aurèle Meissonnier, faithfully reproduced in one of the finest of all western ceramic works, the Swan Service made by Meissen for Count Bruehl in 1737.

Yet if the baroque mood was delayed in its journey northward during the seventeenth century, the rococo was no less fitful in its passage through the European centres of art and craft. By 1780 the Copenhagen factory under Mueller had developed an identifiable national character in its work, and gained a confidence in modelling and decoration which doubtless owed something to the imported skills of Fürstenberg and Meissen. But the mood was sober. There was little evidence – almost half a century after the great essays in frolicsome and fanciful ceramics at Meissen, Vienna and Nymphenburg – of the visual trill, the scroll and the arabesque. Vases with modelled foliage, friezes, symmetrical bases and square plinths reflected the spirit of a past age. The cherubs and angels that surmounted them seemed to owe more to the sculpture of the baroque masters than to the more recent work of Kaendler and Bustelli.

Unfortunately, a just artistic appraisal of the factory's work in the Mueller years (1773-1801) is rendered impossible by the destructive habits of the Danish Court of the time and by a catastrophic fire at the Christiansborg Palace. In the first decade the royal family were by far the most important customers, purchasing something like 13 per cent of the total output, chiefly as gifts for deserving retainers and servants of the State. After 1781, when complete dinner services were first made, a few important purchases were sent abroad as gifts, while other sets – mostly the 'humbler' blue-and-white tableware – were bought for the servants' halls of the several royal palaces of Denmark. Some of the work of the period has thus found its way into private collections and museums.

There is evidence enough to show that Mueller and his artist-craftsmen had mastered the essentials of porcelain manufacture – from the selection and purification of body and glaze ingredients to decoration on and under the glaze and firing in the *grand feu* – within a decade. By the turn of the century they had given Copenhagen wares a distinctive quality which would carry forward the name and reputation of the factory for the succeeding two hundred years.

In 1790 two eccentric French nobles visited the factory in the course of a European tour[29] which took them also to Meissen and other early pottery establishments. Chevalier Louis de Boisgelin and Comte Fortia de Piles were equipped with adequate technical knowledge and they were able to make a useful comparative assessment of the work and methods of Mueller and his colleagues.

There were three large and two small brick kilns, one of them the oven Mueller had used to fire his first experimental pieces seventeen years earlier. The high-temperature gloss firing took 18 hours, followed by a cooling period of four days. 'These ovens are capable of firing eight complete services at once, whereas those of Saxony cannot take in more than three'. The writer adds: 'The fire here is so well distributed that in many of the firings of fine porcelain the loss sustained is scarcely more than ten rixdollars'.

Secrecy, despite the spread of knowledge through Europe by the arcanists of the older factories, was still observed, it seems, in the 1790s. A process described as 'the most important of all', the grinding of the granite (feldspar) and the mixing of paste and glaze, was performed in a room 'where there is only one man, who takes an oath to have no communication whatsoever with any other workman'. The French visitors believed that production was some twelve times that of the Saxony factory. They remarked, too, on the

Factory output at this time was varied. Apart from table and decorative wares, the inventory included bidets, mirrors, clock-dials, knitting pins, buttons, knobs for walking sticks and even musical instruments. And to promote sales, stores were established in Norway, Kiel, Luebeck, Altona, Amsterdam and the Danish West Indies, as well as in Denmark itself. Between 1793 and 1800, 8,845 pieces were shipped to Trondheim. As early as 1785 shipments to Kristiania (Oslo) amounted to 2,875 pieces. Such enterprise was ill rewarded. Goods were often returned unsold and bills frequently remained unpaid.

[28]Diary of John Evelyn in Rome, 1644, quoted in Hillier, *op.cit.*, notes to chapter 'The end of the Baroque'.

[29]See *Travels through Denmark and Sweden etc.* by Louis de Boisgelin, London, 1810, based on *Voyage de deux Francais en Allemagne, Danemarck, Suede, Russie et Pologne, fait en 1790-1792*, par Comte de A.-T.-J.-A.-M.-M. Fortia de Piles, Paris, Desenne, 1796.

ROYAL COPENHAGEN

7 Porcelain dish with indifferently painted landscape, on-glaze, gilt border. Mark in blue. Last quarter eighteenth century. Diameter 7in (177mm). Victoria and Albert Museum, London (The Joicey Bequest).

8 Porcelain chocolate pot and cover, c. 1785. Probably painted by one of the 'Berliners'. Oval medallion on either side, surrounded by floral wreath and containing male and female bust respectively. Painted en grisaille on yellow ground. Handle with gilt imbrications. Height 7½in (190mm). Mark and '1 + 4' incised. Victoria and Albert Museum, London.

THE TRUE PORCELAIN

9 Porcelain tureen and cover, c. 1780. On-glaze enamel decoration with moulding. Mark in blue. Two loop handles in form of stems with floral attachments. Domed cover with similar looped handle. Sides and cover decorated with bunches of flowers and fruit. Height 8½in (216mm), length (overall) 9⅜in (238mm). Victoria and Albert Museum, London.

10 Porcelain cup, cover and stand. Enamel colours and gilding. Mark in underglaze blue and 'K' incised, c. 1780-90. Sides of cup decorated with two medallions with initials 'GB' and 'MB' respectively, partly enclosed by sprays of forget-me-nots. Between them, two lovers in classical costume painted en grisaille. Saucer with wavy rim and painted with medal containing female figure holding hour-glass and bunch of flowers with cockerel at feet. Knob of cover in form of rosebud. Victoria and Albert Museum, London. Cup height 4¾in (121mm), diameter 4in (101mm); saucer diameter 5⅞in (149mm).

quality of the fired wares:

> The Copenhagen porcelain is less glassy than that of China. The paste of the biscuit is lighter and closer to that of the Saxon porcelain, the white keeps its colour better, and it is easier to wash. In short, the whole of this manufacture is perfectly well understood, and carried on with great spirit and diligence. It has only been established thirteen years, and at the end of four the warehouses were already filled with a variety of articles.

They were shown porcelain flutes 'too heavy to be played upon conveniently', and vases 'two and a half feet high most beautifully painted by Camrath'.

These and other visitors of the time reserved their highest praise for the factory's indefatigable manager, doing the work of at least four directors at any of the comparable German or French factories, supervising body and glaze formulations, kilns, modelling, painting and gilding departments. Yet he was, said the Frenchmen, 'shabbily paid', receiving an annual salary of 500 rixdollars, about a third of the value of one of the more elaborate *pot-pourris* of the period. Mueller himself seems to have been less concerned with salary than with the lack of recognition accorded him by the board, in effect Holmskjold the royal proxy. But he was a difficult and exacting man, a scientist who worked, it seems, more by instinct than by instrumentation. In retirement he wrote to one of his successors: 'I fail to see the use or necessity of the thermometer, eudiometer, or hydrometer. I have never found it necessary to apply such exact learning in the manufacture of porcelain, and ideas such as these appear to me to be absolutely absurd'.[30]

Experience had doubtless taught Mueller a lesson that many a ceramic chemist who came after him was to learn by trial and error: that clays and ceramic colours have subtleties of behaviour which can confound scientific theory. Like the Chinese potters of old, he relied more on 'God's finger' than on rational method as a pointer to what might or might not emerge from the kiln.

Whatever his method, Mueller achieved a remarkable level of proficiency in mixing his body and glaze clays, in decoration and firing. Kiln losses were infinitesimal despite the difficulty of maintaining an intense heat of about 1,400 degrees C, from pine logs which had to be cut to ten-feet lengths. And in no area was the factory's output more diverse or impressive than in the production of on-glaze decorated wares which required several firings at different temperatures according to the number and nature of the enamel colours used.

The modelling skills which Luplau brought from Fürstenburg and the decorative expertise imported from Meissen were undoubted assets in the early years. But Mueller's mastery of the chemistry of the porcelain clays and the metal oxides employed in decoration, and his purposeful direction of every aspect of his team's work, both technical and artistic, were crucial factors. So too were the contributions of native artists. The sculptor Claus Tvede joined the factory in 1775 and though his work is not identified he is believed to have contributed significantly to a number of figure models attributed to others. Jacob Schmidt, another modeller of note, joined the factory at the age of 14 in 1779. A year later two exceptional artists joined the modelling department: G. Kalleberg and J. J. Holm. The latter became model-master in his last year at the factory, 1802. Nicolai Abildgaard, director of the Danish Royal Academy, was appointed artistic adviser.

There was an influx of outstanding portrait and landscape artists too in the 1770s. Hans Clio contributed several signed landscapes to the factory's porcelain and acted as drawing-master to trainees. Lars Hansen arrived in 1777 and became a master of underglaze blue decoration. Hans Christoph Ondrup; Peter Lehmann; Johannes Ludwig and F. C. Camradt; Nicolai Christian Faxoe; Soren Preus; Elias Meyer and M. Meyer; N. Bau; Carl Friedrich Thomaschevsky (who came from the Berlin factory with Lehmann in 1780); Raben Svardalyn; Hans Jacob Hansen; Christian Ahrensborg; Matthias Wolstrup: these and many others contributed their varied, and sometimes varying, skills to the decoration of large-scale 'royal' vases and *pot-pourris*, to everyday wares in on-glaze enamels and underglaze blue, figures, and even, as we have seen, musical instruments in porcelain. But of all the artists who came on the scene in the primordial years, none was to make a greater impact on the long-term fame of the Copenhagen manufactory than the German Johan Christoph Bayer. A landscape painter from Nuremberg, he entered the service of Mueller's factory on 16 November 1776. Holmskjold, the proxy of the royal owner on

[30] Mueller to Boyle, quoted in Hayden, *op.cit.*, p.67.

11 *Vase with lid. Medallion portrait of King Christian VII*, c. 1780-85. Height 10¼in (260mm). Royal Copenhagen Museum.

THE TRUE PORCELAIN

11

ROYAL COPENHAGEN

12 *Start of a tradition of fine enamel-decorated punch bowls marking historic events – detail from the Battle of Copenhagen bowl commissioned after the famous naval engagement by U. W. de Roepsdorff, retired Governor-General of the Danish West Indies. Forty-four were made, the last of them in 1807, for presentation to Danish officers who took part. They show battle scenes with the Dannebrog flying and bear the inscription:*
   Dedicated to O. Fischer and all the brave Danes. Copenhagen, 2 April 1801, from Roepsdorff.
Royal Copenhagen Museum.

the board of the company, was a distinguished naturalist and Bayer undertook the illustration of his book on Danish fungi. He was to undertake, also, one of the most painstaking and exhaustive tasks in the entire history of European porcelain: the decoration of a royal service of immense size and variety of shape with the flora of his adopted country. Minute attention to detail would be its hallmark. In the course of time Flora Danica would become the most distinguished, and probably the most costly, of essays in western ceramics.

Mueller's twenty-six year reign as factory manager was dogged by dissension within the royal family and by the economic vicissitudes that flowed from the Napoleonic wars and the politically unsettled state of Europe at the end of the eighteenth century. He was a man of unbending resolution and if he enabled the Royal Copenhagen manufactory to become productive and to achieve a high level of technical and artistic excellence in the face of dissolute ownership, his determined manner also gave rise to ill feeling. There was much work and little concord in the Mueller years. Following the overthrow and banishment of Queen Juliane Marie and her son Frederik in 1784, the Crown Prince Frederik became Regent to the demented Christian VII, and Holmskjold the Privy Councillor became the

13 *Another view of the Battle of Copenhagen bowl showing Danish men-of-war attacking Nelson's ships. Executed from drawing by C. A. Lorentzen, 1806-7. Royal Copenhagen Museum.*

sole director of the factory, a fact which might be supposed to have strengthened the hand of Mueller who had married his sister. It was not a helpful alliance, however. The proud manager and the socially superior director seldom saw eye to eye. The widower Mueller married Holm's elderly sister Anna Catherine on 7 January 1780. But the parlous state of the country's finances and the economies which the board forced on Mueller brought the two men into constant conflict. On Holmskjold's death in 1793 it was discovered that he had misappropriated the factory's funds, and a commission appointed to look into the matter decided that the factory should in future be administered by the Royal Postal Department. Mueller was made 'artistic director', and Peter Grönland (later director) was made company secretary.

The old Queen died in retirement in 1796. Mueller retired in 1801, the year of the Battle of Copenhagen when Nelson's fleet fought its costly but victorious engagement with the Danish navy. The porcelain factory by the Round Tower remained intact for a few more years, which was long enough to complete its greatest work.

History's most bitter moments are often recorded in the afterthought, the *beau geste*. Soon after the famous battle of 2 April 1801, Nelson wrote to Lady Hamilton, whose cuckolded husband had stimulated the all-enveloping wave of neo-classicism at Wedgwood's Etruria:

> My dear Friend,
> I was in hopes that I should get off some Copenhagen china to have sent you by Captain Bligh, who was one of my seconds on the 2nd. . . .

That letter was dated 14 April. The next day

ROYAL COPENHAGEN

he wrote again to Emma, in slightly more affectionate tone:

> My dearest friend,
> I can get nothing here worth your acceptance, but as I know you have a valuable collection of china, I send you some of the Copenhagen manufacture. It will bring to your recollection that here your friend Nelson fought and conquered. Captain Bligh has promised to take charge of it, and I hope it will reach you safe. . . . Ever yours, most faithfully, NELSON AND BRONTE.

The sea battle of 1801 was preceded by a disastrous fire at Christiansborg in 1794 and further conflagrations in 1795 which destroyed almost a quarter of the city. As if those events were not sufficiently destructive, British forces reappeared in 1807 to complete the

14 *Royal Copenhagen's bicentenary bowl, issued in limited edition of 2,500 in 1975. Waterfront motif designed by Sven Vestergaard and painted by Finn Clausen. Elsinore Castle (Kronborg) on right. Royal Copenhagen Museum.*

THE TRUE PORCELAIN

demolition. The porcelain factory was bombarded and hundreds of moulds for the original creations of Mueller's time were left beneath the rubble. The factory marked the battle of Copenhagen with a commemorative bowl which paid tribute to the brave Danes who fell at sea. Richly decorated and dated 2 April 1801, it became the prototype of finely decorated bowls which, over succeeding centuries, would record the laudable and sanguinary events of the world.

In 1808 the Crown Prince Frederik succeeded his imbecile father Christian VII on the Danish throne. Mueller, who had witnessed in retirement the physical destruction of the factory he built, lived to see its artistic decline in the reign of the new monarch. He died on 4 March 1820 in his 88th year.

15 *American War of Independence bowl, in limited edition of 2,500, featuring Washington at Battle of Princeton, English frigates on the Hudson, contemporary coat of arms and date 1776. Height 5¾in (148mm), diameter 13¹/₁₆in (332mm). Artist, Sven Vestergaard, 1976.*

3
The Royal Vases
The Rosenborg Palace Collection

AMONG the most important wares of the Queen Juliane Marie Period were numerous vases with elaborate decoration in the form of painted friezes and portraits, modelled flowers and human and anthropomorphic figures, 'sprigged' foliage, and gilt and enamel ornamentation. They were the products of the factory most to the taste of the royal family. Despite a considerable demand for table services for the many royal palaces, records show that only one complete service was purchased by the King up to the year 1803, and one each by Queen Juliane Marie, the Crown Prince and the Heir Presumptive. Of the palace collections, only a small number of vases remain to remind us of the factory's most ambitious and painstaking early work; and they survive by a near miracle of rescue.

Fire broke out at the Christiansborg Palace in the afternoon of Wednesday 26 February, 1794. By nightfall many of the rarest art treasures of Europe had been reduced to charred

THE ROYAL VASES

remains. Among those treasures were almost all the best pieces from Mueller's years of dedicated and inspired porcelain making. They were destroyed along with paintings, sculpture, tapestries and other furnishings which represented one of the great collections of Oriental and European art. Perhaps, too, some of the surviving wares of the old Fournier factory were lost in the fire.

Eleven of the royal pieces from Christiansborg were rescued: a bust of Queen Juliane Marie and ten vases. They were placed for safe keeping in the Rosenborg Palace where they remain to the present day. In them we see echoes of the baroque, of the modelled angels and cherubs of Bernini and Soldani-Benzi which the Italian Doccia factory made into fine ceramic sculpture in the 1740s. We see, too, an almost whispered rendering of the art of the *rocailleurs*, shell-encrustation, and of the *style pittoresque*, but always subdued and disciplined, never breaking out into the true flippancy of unrestrained rococo art. And we see the new classicism which Sir William Hamilton had introduced to Wedgwood[31] at the new Etruria in the 1760s, but painted *en grisaille* rather than moulded in the popular manner of the reliefs of the great English potter. Copenhagen porcelain in its first period was never revolutionary. Its important feature was an implicit national style; a characteristic vein of artistry which ran through the predominant styles of European art and craft, unassertively, almost imperceptibly, becoming in the course of time the corner-stone of the factory's world-wide fame and of Danish eminence in the applied and decorative arts.

The ten large and cumbersome pieces, miraculously rescued from the fire at Christiansborg along with the bust of the Queen (see frontispiece and fig. 54), despite the panic and confusion which reigned, deserve a detailed appraisal:

[31] Flaxman exhibited two wax models for portraits, and a figure of Neptune, at Royal Academy in 1770. Accepted offer to work for Wedgwood and Bentley 1775.

The factory records for 23 November 1780 list '2 potpourri jars with figures on the lid holding a flower basket with black-painted emblems in medallion, variegated flowers, gold lace edging of virgin paste, best Ondrup ware. For the Queen'. An entry in the sales ledger, of the same date, records: '2 large smelling jars/Por Porri (sic)/variegated flowers and gold ornament and medals painted with hunting scenes in black at 50 rixdollars apiece'.

These matter-of-fact entries conceal technical and artistic details of some significance. 'Virgin paste', for example, refers to the use of French kaolin, although native Bornolm clays were still in use as the principal ingredients of the porcelain body mix. In 1778 Mueller had imported an initial four barrels of the whiter and purer clays from the St. Yrieix deposits in France, but they were used only experimentally and for special decorative features prior to 1781. The use of the term 'best ware', meaning first grade, indicates the production of lower-grade utility wares (chiefly blue painted) in the porcelain body at this time; many of them for the use of servants in the royal palaces but others, presumably, for public purchase in the Kobmagergade shop. H. C. Ondrup, the painter, was one of the factory's best artists of the period. The motif in the oval medallion is taken from a print by J. E. Ridinger, dated 1756. On the reverse medallion is a hunting trophy painted by Ondrup from a print by G.-F. Riedel after C. Huet. The lid is held closed by a groove under the openwork edge.

Source: Grandjean, *op.cit.*, p. 18-20.

---

16 Front and rear of so-called pot-pourri *vase, one of pair, with closed, perforated cover. Decorated by H. C. Ondrup in 1780, and purchased by Queen Juliane Marie in same year. Height 14⅛ in (360mm). Saved from fire at Christiansborg Palace in 1794. Rosenborg Palace Collection, Copenhagen.*

31

ROYAL COPENHAGEN

THE ROYAL VASES

Vase described as *pot-pourri* with extra internal lid, modelled flowers and foliage, and portrait of Crown Prince Frederik painted *en grisaille* by F. C. Camradt from engraving by J. F. Clemens executed in 1784 after the painting by Jens Juel. Text on rear of vase FREDERICUS CHRISTIANI VII REGIS DANIAE FILIUS REGNI HAERES. No date included, but known to be 1784 from factory records. More slender and elegantly shaped than the Ondrup vase, and one of the most beautiful of the royal portrait vessels. Its delicately entwined decoration on lid and foot is repeated in two other vases, perhaps forming part of set, bearing portraits of Princess Louise Augusta and Queen Juliane Marie, also saved from the Christiansborg fire. It is likely that Camradt completed the decoration of all three vases before 1786.

Note that rocailles handles of the Ondrup vase are replaced by simple gilded branches contiguous with sprig decoration. Superior figure, as on other Rosenborg Collection vases, has distinct resemblance to Fürstenberg infant figures of period, perhaps modelled by Luplau.

17 *Vase with extra internal lid, modelled flowers and portrait of Crown Prince Frederik painted* en grisaille *by F. C. Camradt in 1784 after an engraving by J. F. Clemens. Height 18in (460mm). Saved from Christiansborg fire. Rosenborg Palace Collection, Copenhagen.*

18 *Vase similar to that shown in fig. 17, but with maladroit figure surmounting lid. Also extra internal lid, and portrait medallion of Crown Prince Frederik (King of Denmark 1808-39). Mark and 'K' incised. Reverse inscription as on other version. Overall height 18in (464mm). Purchased in 1881 by Victoria and Albert Museum, London, source anonymous. A similar vase in the Kunstindustri-museum, Copenhagen, is dated 1785.*

Source: Grandjean, *op.cit.*, p.20. See also his *Kongelig Dansk Porcelain*, Thanning & Appel, Copenhagen, 1962.

ROYAL COPENHAGEN

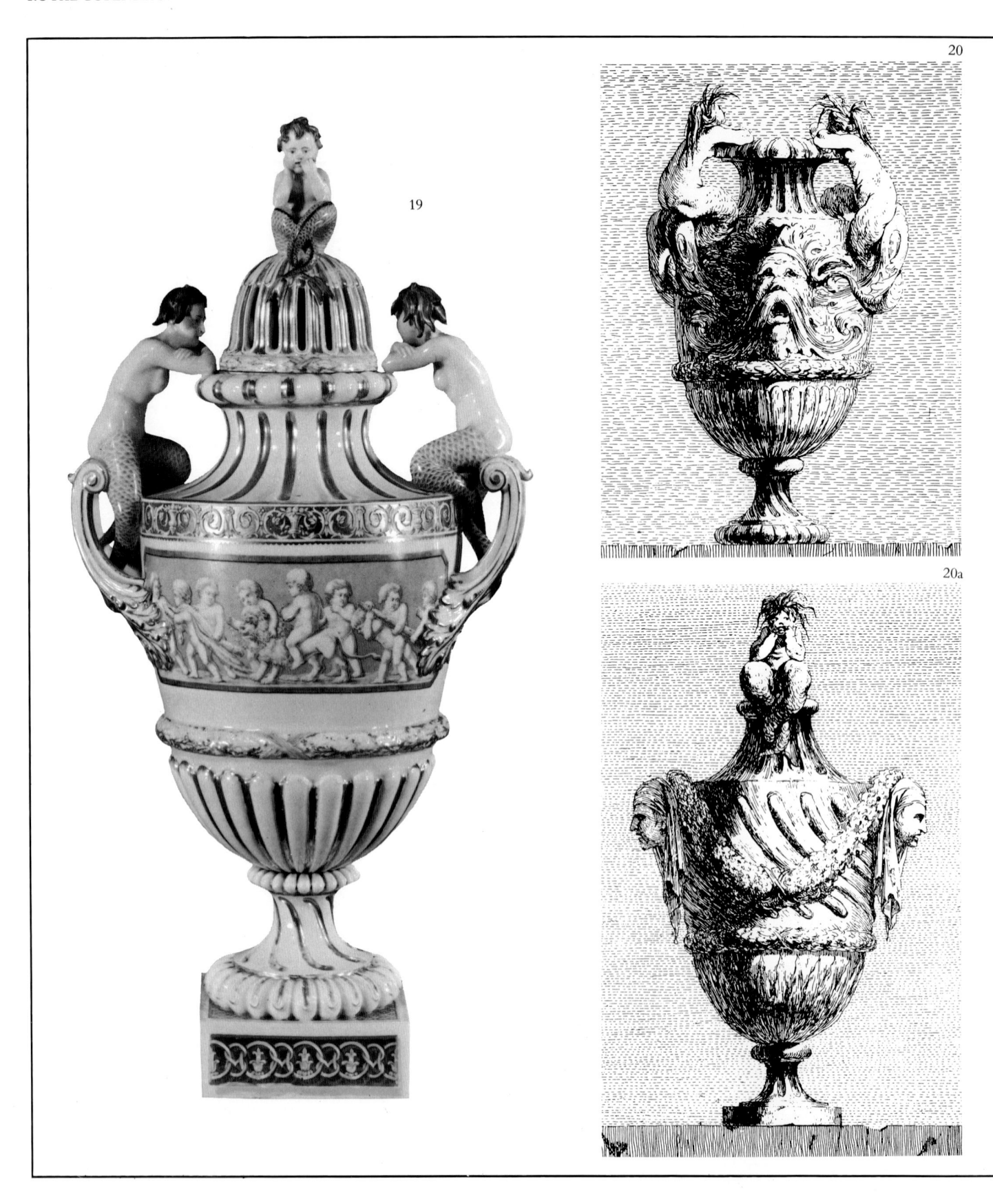

34

Vase sold to Crown Prince on New Year's Eve 1788 for 300 rixdollars, a sum equal to the average yearly wage of a porcelain decorator. Modelled from etchings by J.-F.-J. Saly, frieze painted *en grisaille* with allegory based on Hercules myth.

   Saly, an outstanding artist of the French neo-classical movement, supplied a number of 'ornament prints' and at least one figure theme (*see* p. 75) to the Copenhagen factory. The prints shown opposite are clearly the foundation of this 'mermaid' vase. The unknown designer of the vase has reduced Saly's wild and fanciful concept to conformity with the decorative style of the architect Harsdorff in Danish interiors such as those of the Fredensborg Palace. To quote Grandjean in his 200th anniversary monograph on the factory: 'the form has been cleansed, all the wildness somehow blown away. The lovely, amorous sea-nymphs have been transformed into two provincial students listening to a lecture, and the little rascal of a sea-boy into a goody-goody doll. . . . fruity baroque has become bloodless classicism'. This was probably the first of a series of large-scale works commanded by Holmskjold in the hope of tempting the Crown Prince, in the years following the economic depression of 1784-88. Numerous examples of the same vase were produced between the years 1788 and 1807.

Source: Grandjean, *op.cit.*, p.21.

19 *Vase modelled from etchings by J.-F.-J. Saly, with friezes painted* en grisaille, *1788. Height 32in (820mm). Rescued from Christiansborg fire. Rosenborg Palace Collection, Copenhagen.*

20 and 20a *Etchings for vase by Saly.*

ROYAL COPENHAGEN

21

Vase entered in factory books August 1789, closely resembling a model from Fürstenberg. Described as 'large Antique vase with figure on lid and flower festoon, ornamented with yellow and green gold and engraved'. The Fürstenberg original was first produced at the time Luplau moved to Copenhagen, and it is likely that the German model-master was responsible for this fine piece, perhaps working from memory. The Copenhagen version is of more graceful proportion than its counterpart, being slightly flattened in the vertical plane, and it demonstrates the excellence of the paste which Mueller had achieved by this time with his 'Virgin clay' containing a very high percentage of French kaolin. The term 'antique' refers in particular to the beautifully designed handles in the form of goats' heads holding a festoon in their mouths: a familiar Roman and neo-classical device, but here achieving a relevance to the overall design seldom found in contemporary work. Moulds for this vase were destroyed in 1807 and a list of damage sustained in that fateful year mentions 'mould for large oval vase with figure and ram's head for handle', and 'boy for oval vase'.

Source: Grandjean, *op.cit.*, p.22.

21 Vase copied and slightly reworked from Fürstenberg model, 1789. Probably modelled by Luplau. Height 31½in (800mm). Rescued from Christiansborg fire. Rosenborg Palace Collection, Copenhagen.

22

Vase with two Fama figures and decoration *en grisaille* with acanthus leaves and classical heads in medallions, 1789. In terms of size and complexity the most important and ambitious project attempted by Mueller's workmen and artists; and the most expensive item of the period, being purchased by the Crown Prince as a birthday present to himself in 1790 for 1,500 rixdollars. Contemporary newspaper reports[32] on the vase prompted Mueller to make a public pronouncement commending the work for 'the quality of the material, the excellence of the work, and the beauty of the decoration, but especially on account of its unusual size'. The factory manager's enthusiasm for the size of the work cannot be gainsaid. Artistically it has an ambivalent quality. Horizontal sections heavily demarcated by wreaths destroy the flow of gadrooning and fluting at neck and foot. The Fama figures, on the other hand, with trumpets and flowing robes, are eloquent echoes of baroque sculptural themes. Medallion heads of Apollo and Minerva are copied from prints in Philippe de Stosch's catalogue of European private collections, published in 1724, a book much used by the factory's painters.

[32] *Altonaischer Mercurius*, 4 Feb., 1790; Odense, *Adressekontors Efterretninger*, 9 Feb.; Mueller, *ibid*, 12 Feb.

Source: Grandjean, *op.cit.*, p.22-3.

22 *Vase with two Fama (Famous: classical mythology) figures, Apollo and Minerva, decorated* en grisaille; *acanthus leaves and two medallions with antique heads, 1789. Bought by Crown Prince Frederik in 1790. Height 46½in (1180mm). Saved from Christiansborg fire. Rosenborg Palace Collection, Copenhagen.*

ROYAL COPENHAGEN

23

40

Vase or flowerpot, decorated *en grisaille* with scene of marriage of Amor and Psyche. One of pair modelled in 1789, purchased by Crown Prince Frederik in 1790. Made from main mould used for big 'Fama' vase. Entered in factory books as '2 Flowerpots painted with Figures and ornamented with Arabesques'. Priced at 450 rixdollars each. Painted motif is allusion to wedding of young Prince which took place in July 1790. Amor (Cupid) and Psyche are shown as a child bridal couple with their heads swathed being led by a string of beads held by Hymen to the marriage bed. The allegorical illustration is taken from a print in de Stosch's catalogue.[33] On the back of the vase is painted an altar or pedestal with a royal throne and, at the foot, a quiver, a torch and a laurel wreath. Lions' masks on the base suggest that pedestals were supplied for mounting the vases at Christiansborg Palace.

23 Vase or flowerpot (one of pair), modelled 1789. Decorated en grisaille *with scene from wedding of Amor (Cupid) and Psyche. Bought by Crown Prince Frederik in 1790. Height 31¾in (810mm). Saved from Christiansborg fire. Rosenborg Palace Collection, Copenhagen.*

[33] The work on which the painted allegory of this vase is based is the subject of the famous 'Marlborough gem' carved in sardonyx, and is known in other representations, e.g. a drawing by G. B. Cipriani reproduced in Jacob Bryant's *A New System, or an analysis of ancient Mythology*, vol. 1, 1775, and again engraved by Fr. Bartolozzi in the catalogue of the Duke of Marlborough's collection, vol. 1, 1780. The ornament engraver M. A. Pergolesi also used the engraving, incorporated in a print of grotesque decorations published 1777. And Wedgwood had the gem copied in jasperware (1773) and modelled by Flaxman in 1778 *(Marriage of Cupid and Psyche)* with companions (*Cupids with Goat* and *A Sacrifice to Hymen*). See Tattersall, 'Flaxman and Wedgwood' in RA Catalogue, October 1979.

Source: Grandjean, *op.cit.*, p.26.

4
Early On-glaze Enamelled Wares

FORTUNATELY the sumptuous vases of the Queen Juliane Marie period were deemed unsuitable for the rebuilt Christiansborg Palace, designed by C. F. Hansen in 1803-28 in the neo-classical vogue. Had they been incorporated in that building their charmed life would almost certainly have failed to survive a second hazard, for the palace was completely destroyed in another fire in 1884. As it is, they remain to the present day as testimony to the varied skills and the high artistry of Mueller's team. But they are essentially royal pieces, made to impress benefactors and princely customers: elaborate, sometimes over-elaborate, in decoration and modelling, paying lip service to the new classicism and allying its rich mythology to the still pervasive influences of baroque *art grotesque* and rococo *joie de vivre*.

Mueller's workforce grew rapidly during the last three decades of the eighteenth century. By 1781 it numbered approximately 200; by 1790, 300, some 40 of whom were engaged in painting. From 1790 the financial position of the factory had been more or less secured by a Customs regulation which forbade the importation of foreign porcelain, except that 'brought over by the East India ships belonging to the Asiatic Company'. The regulation also prohibited the importation of painted earthenware, 'its resemblance to porcelain[34] being so great that many may be induced to purchase it instead of a more valuable article'.

Plain earthenware was allowed, however, for the use of the lower classes. Even the lesser products of the royal factory were clearly intended for the rich. But it was in these, tableware and decorative items for the servants' quarters of the royal households and wealthy commoners, that Mueller's artists demonstrated the versatility of their talents and superimposed on the styles and decorative themes of their age a national idiom which derived from Danish folk art, from a keen and sympathetic observation of landscape, of flora and fauna and of ordinary people. Sentiment was a pronounced feature of the decorative work of the on-glaze decorators with their multi-colour palettes; but not sentimentality. From its very inception the Copenhagen factory avoided the banalities inherent in artistic precocity and in brazen commercialism. Sometimes naive, even dull, the utility and decorative wares nevertheless avoided the sin of pretentiousness. Honest workmanship and a native urbanity which was capable of uniting the universal with the vernacular in its design philosophy, set Copenhagen apart from its competitors at an early stage.

The Frenchmen de Boisgelin and de Piles noted some of the technicalities of enamel decoration in 1790, and they paid passing tribute to Mueller's pragmatic but effective chemistry. Yellow, they observed, was made from tin; purple from tin and gold, dark poppy from iron, sky-blue from cobalt, black from manganese, rose-colour from gold, green from copper. 'These colours never change in firing, but remain precisely as first drawn; whereas they spread in many other factories.' It was not by any means a scientific account of decorating either under or on the glaze. In Mueller's time, indeed until very recent times, the metal oxides used in ceramic painting demanded the most careful purification and mixing, and firing at precisely calculated temperatures with primitively controlled air flow to ensure the correct degree of reduction or oxidation. Artistry and technique vacillated in quality and assurance. Disasters in the decorating kiln were not common at Copenhagen: but they were not unknown. However, the Frenchmen's account gives some idea of the factory's scope and inventiveness.

[34] Hayden, *op.cit.*, p.76, translates phrase as 'resemblance to china'.

Early On-glaze Enamelled Wares

24 *Huntsman with hound on octagonal dish. Blue border with gold tracery, c. 1780-90. Dansk Folke Museum, Copenhagen.*

25 *Sucrier and cover, decorated with deep blue bands and elaborate gilding, and panel with harvest figure inscribed 'Guds Frucht'. Rosebud handle on lid, c. 1780-90. Dansk Folke Museum, Copenhagen.*

26 *Saucer decorated with eagle and lamb. Gilded border, c. 1780-90. Kunstindustrimuseum, Copenhagen.*

27 and 27a *Snuff-box made in 1777. Enamel decoration by C. D. Luplau, brother of the model master (at Copenhagen 1776-78), based on Danish scenes on outside, and allegorical figure within. Factory mark on inside of base. Damaged lid. Overall length 4¼in (110mm). Royal Copenhagen Museum.*

5
Flora Danica

THE Flora Danica service, work on which began in 1790, is unique in the annals of porcelain manufacture. Its name has become synonymous with the title of the botanical encyclopedia, published between the years 1761 and 1883, on which it is based. For nearly 200 years attempts have been made in many parts of the world to emulate and plagiarise this masterly work of Danish applied art. None has even remotely succeeded.

The artistic intention implicit in the decoration of this vast service was the accurate rendering of the country's plant life, choosing those botanical specimens most suited to portrayal on the variously shaped surfaces of hundreds of individual pieces, in compositions which were aesthetically pleasing. But what can have been the commercial purpose of so ambitious a project, at a factory which was far from wealthy at the time of its inception and certainly in no position to indulge itself in whims?

One tradition, almost as old as the service itself, is that it was made for that renowned patron of the arts the Empress Catherine II of Russia. There is no substantial evidence that the Empress ever ordered a single piece of Copenhagen porcelain or that the Danish Regent of the time, the Crown Prince Frederik, ever intended to present such a service to her. Most historians of the Royal Manufactory are inclined to the view that the origins of the service are obscure and shrouded in uncertainty. One of them, however, the English writer and popular art historian Arthur Hayden, is unequivocal: 'In 1790 the *Flora Danica* service was ordered by the Crown Prince. It was not at first known for whom it was intended. The old factory books record it as "Perle model broget malet med *Flora Danica*" (Pearl body, colour painted with *Flora Danica*). As the service progressed it transpired that it was to be presented to Catherine II, Empress of Russia.' Hayden is unreliable. He offers no evidence for his statement, which is probably guesswork. Yet his conjecture could contain an element of truth. It is possible that the Crown Prince or his advisers saw in the presentation of so magnificent a service an opportunity to cement relations with imperial Russia, which had depended since 1773 on a non-aggression pact directed against Sweden. If so, Privy Councillor Holmskjold, combining the roles of royal adviser, factory director and distinguished naturalist, would have lost no time in informing his brother-in-law Mueller of the Regent's notion. It may be safely assumed that Holmskjold would have given the idea his enthusiastic backing. Yet if the service was conceived in 1790 it must be conceded that the need to placate the Russian Empress had diminished somewhat. That year a binding peace with Sweden was concluded, and the need for the assistance of the imperial Russian navy, often at anchor in Danish waters, had receded.

There can be little doubt, however, that the idea of a presentation of the service to Catherine II would have occurred at some time to the factory hierarchy. After all, the presentation of the Wedgwood Creamware (or 'Queensware') service to the Empress in 1774, and of the Sèvres table service in the *pâte tendre* four years later, made a powerful impact on European potters in general. Certainly Wedgwood made no effort in correspondence with business associates to hide the fact that he had wooed the Russian Court assiduously in order to obtain the commission for nearly a thousand pieces decorated with English landscapes and noble residences.[35] Neither did he conceal his concern for the commercial advantages that would accrue from the Empress's patronage.

An almost certain, if negative, reason for disbelieving the story of a commission by the Empress resides in the fact that there is no official correspondence in the Danish archives suggesting that the ambassador at the Peterhof, Niels Rosenkrantz, ever broached the subject of a porcelain service.[36]

[35] See monograph: *The Imperial Russian Dinner Service*, by Dr G. C. Williamson, Bell, London, 1909; and Mankowitz, Wolf, *Wedgwood*, Spring Books, 1966, p.47, Wedgwood to Thomas Bentley, 23 March, 1773, 'service for my Great Patroness in the North'.

[36] See Grandjean, *The Flora Danica Service*, Forum, Copenhagen, 1973, note 6.

28 *Plate from the original Flora Danica service, c. 1790. Diameter 9in (230mm). Royal Copenhagen Museum.*

FLORA DANICA

28

45

ROYAL COPENHAGEN

Even the date of the inception of work on the service is in doubt. In April 1788 Johan Bülow, the Lord Chamberlain, visited the factory in order to 'inspect the things ordered by the Crown Prince'. The sales journal records that on 2 July 1788 the Crown Prince received a dinner service of many colours. It has been deduced that these references were to the Flora Danica service.[37]

It cannot have been so. A memorandum by Mueller dated 6 March 1792 states unequivocally that work on 'the large commissioned dinner service, painted with flowers after *Flora Danica*', lasted rather more than two years. That would suggest that work started early in 1790. A private document, the diary of Dr. F. V. P. Fabricius in the Rönne Museum, seems to offer confirmation of the date and support for the 'Empress' theory.[38] One of Mueller's sons was staying at the home of Fabricius in 1794, and a handwritten note in the diary for that year quotes the young Mueller as saying: 'Sie machte gegenwärtig ein Porzelans Service zu 100 Couverts mit der Flora Danica auf zu der kayserin, welche 40,000 Rdlr. koste'.

The young man exaggerated the cost of the service and he was probably guessing at the number of persons for whom it was intended. It was not until 1797 that a decision was made to increase the number of place-settings from 80 to 100. All the same, the evidence of father and son seems to point irrefutably to 1790 as the starting point. In that year the French visitors de Piles and de Boisgelin noted the Flora Danica service but 'on ignorait encore, lorsque nous l'avons vu, à qui il était destiné'.[39] And on Saturday 28 August, 1790, a small item of expenditure in the factory records reveals that on that day a manservant was sent to Kobermager Street by the librarian to King Christian VII with a copy of the *Flora Danica* botanical work. He was paid 4 Rigsdaler for his pains.[40]

In all probability the Crown Prince, who made most of the decisions of the Court during his Regency, conceived the idea at some time of presenting the service to the Russian Empress, perhaps in the conceptual stage before 1790, but later abandoned the idea. In any case, the death of Catherine in 1796 resolved the problem, if it existed, of deciding the destination of the great work. The Crown Prince Frederik was happy to take possession of it.

In 1783 Christian VII bought a dinner service which was decorated with medallions containing *putti* in clouds, painted in grey and mauve from engravings by Daullé (after Fr. Boucher), and surrounded by floral wreaths. It consisted of 306 pieces, together with a table mirror, and was composed of 21 different models. It was almost certainly in the 'pearl' design, and may have been similar to the dinner service ordered by the Crown Prince which Bülow inspected in 1788. The name 'pearl' is derived from the row of pearls, each fixed separately in relief, which is found as a border on each piece. The design was chosen for Flora Danica because it was considered best suited to a royal service, although 61 new models had to be created as work progressed. Reference to the pearl design first appears in the factory records in 1783. Like Auliczek's pearl service[41] for Nymphenburg, the Copenhagen version retains touches of the rococo spirit in its handles with modelled flowers and foliage, but its disc ornament, labelled 'ducat ornament' by Chr. A. Jensen, is classical in origin, and the relief borders give it a Louis-Seize flavour.[42]

The decoration of the Flora Danica service was to be the life's work of one of the most gifted and sensitive artists of the late eighteenth century, and one of the greatest of ceramic painters, Johann Christoph Bayer. When he joined the factory in November 1776 he was the first qualified painter in Mueller's team. He had been invited to Copenhagen eight years earlier by G. Chr. Oeder, the publisher of *Flora Danica*. His drawing of plants was masterly, and his skill was further exemplified in his work for Holmskjold's definitive book on Danish fungi, *Beata ruris otia fungis danicis impensa*, the first part of which was published in 1790.

29 *Johann Christoph Bayer, from a contemporary engraving.*

[37] Administrative correspondence, 1788, cited in Grandjean, *ibid*. See Karl Madsen in *Tidsskrift for Kunstindustri*, 1893.

[38] Grandjean, *op.cit.*, p.12.

[39] *Voyage de deux Francais*, Vol.1, p.302.

[40] Factory archive. See Grandjean, *op.cit.*, p.10.

[41] c.1792-5

[42] Grandjean, *op.cit.*, p.12, note 13.

Bayer's skill was matched by his versatility and by his humility. He contributed during his first 14 years at the factory to both underglaze blue decorated wares and to the less constrained work of on-glaze enamelling. Every decorative process, it seems, presented a challenge to his considerable talents and nothing was too insignificant to command their application. When it came to the painting of the Flora Danica service, of which he decorated the vast majority of 1,802 pieces in the course of eleven years, verisimilitude was the paramount requirement. Exact copying of the book illustrations, many of which were his own, was demanded. If detailed characteristics of botanical specimens were in doubt, actual plants were obtained from the Botanical Gardens to ensure the correctness of the most minute features in the porcelain rendering. Many of the factory artists regarded such slavish application as beneath their dignity. Bayer accepted the discipline without qualm. He gave his mature years to the task and expended all his strength on it. At the end he was almost blind, and so weakened physically that he was beyond recovery. He created a monument to his own genius, to the Royal Manufactory and to ceramic art.

Since moulds already existed for the pearl pattern used for a large number of individual pieces, work was doubtless begun on the decoration of Flora Danica as soon as the royal commission was received. There would, in any case, have been undecorated pearl-ware in stock. Presumably the task of modelling and making engraved moulds for new pieces – a long and laborious process – began at the same time. Heavily decorated handles were modelled by hand, as were the innumerable moulded flowers which were made by the modeller Soren Preuss.[43] Shaping and turning, cutting out rims, perforation (much lacework was included in the designs), glazing, firing, decoration with carefully mixed and graded rust colours, gilding, and subsequent firings in the decorating kilns: the processes were long drawn-out and meticulously supervised by Mueller himself. All this was in addition to maintaining the factory's normal production. Opportunity was taken to produce some pearl-design porcelain over and above the requirements of the Flora Danica service, which was decorated with fruit and flowers. Some was sold undecorated.[44]

Records relating to the progress of the service are rare, but an idea of the enthusiasm and labour of the first few years can be gained from the counts that were made of individual pieces. In September 1792 it was calculated that 988 pieces had been completed, along with 54 figures. The latter – according to the evidence of the French visitors[45] in 1790 – probably resulted from an original intention to include figures with national costumes and military uniforms, an idea which was quickly abandoned.

The next count, in November 1794, showed a total of 1,351 pieces. There was no mention of figures. Thus, 988 pieces (many modelled from scratch) made and decorated in the first two years were followed by 363 pieces in the following two years. The disparity is partly explained by the fact that of the earlier output 175 items consisted of knife handles, 80 of custard cups, and 12 of salt cellars, none of which required elaborate decoration. Another factor may have been the availability of ready cast and fired pearl-wares early on.[46]

Work came almost to a standstill between November 1794 and September 1797, during which time only 81 pieces were completed. On 7 September 1797 it was decided to increase the number of place settings from 80 to 100, after which date 370 new pieces were painted. On 7 July 1802 a Palace edict, issued by the Crown Prince on behalf of the King, stated: 'It is Our desire that work should cease on the Flora Danica service destined for Us'. The order was obeyed punctiliously. Four of the cruets finally delivered to the Palace with the service were never to have accompanying

30 *Fish strainer and dish from original Flora Danica service, with moulded trout handle on strainer painted in natural colours. Dish decoration shows somewhat slavish adherence to book illustrations characteristic of some early pieces. Rosenborg Palace Collection, Copenhagen.*

[43] At factory 1784–1801.

[44] See Grandjean, *op.cit.*, note 18.

[45] '*Le service representera aussi les coustumes des differens peuples soumis a la domination danoise, et les uniformes des troupes*', de Piles, *op.cit.*

[46] Hayden, *op.cit.*, says (p.143): 'in 1794 no less than 1,835 pieces were ready', a figure which exceeds the total number of pieces in the completed service. Karl Madsen, *Tidsskrift for Kunstindustri*, 1893, speaks of 2,528 pieces at a stock-taking in 1797; the actual number was 1,432. The historian Emil Hannover inherited the mistake in *Keramisk Haandbog*, see Grandjean, *op.cit.*, note 20.

Note on botanical illustrations: The general rule was to paint large plants and botanical features on large vessels, plates etc, and small subjects on small items of porcelain. But there are many exceptions. Volumes of the book *Flora Danica* were being produced as the service progressed so that it was impossible to plan a scheme of decoration; and in 1797 supplements to the botanical work were commissioned, thus extending the choice of illustrations for the modellers and decorators. Here and there items of the service are inappropriately decorated, e.g. a large tureen with a few thin stems, or a small dish almost entirely covered by a singe fungus. Horizontal and vertical devices are also sometimes used indiscriminately. There must be a suspicion that Bayer was not entirely a free agent. It is quite possible that his work was subject to censorship over the long period of work on the service, and at times there may have been adjudication by committee. See Grandjean, *op.cit.*, p.48.

[47] About £3,000 sterling, or $12,000 at the time.

[48] Moltke Palace was one of four royal households known collectively as Amalienborg, in Frederiksstaden. The Crown Prince lived in the Schack Palace, connected by a passageway to Moltke Palace.

[49] Correspondence in factory archive, 30 Nov. 1802.

[50] Royal archive, correspondence Hofmarskallatets Archiv.

dishes. The price of the service which was entered in the factory books was 23,224 Rigsdaler (Rixdollars).[47]

Only one artist other than Bayer is known to have contributed to the Flora Danica service, Christian Nicolai Faxoe. Between the years 1799 and 1800 he painted, gilded and ornamented 158 pieces, and ornamented and gilded another 15. It is possible that Faxoe came on the scene when Bayer's eyesight was failing; it is unlikely that he worked on the service prior to 1799.

The quality of both botanical illustration and modelling is uneven, though the fact is hardly surprising in view of the immensity of the task, the long period over which it was executed and the gradual deterioration of its chief artist's health and sight.

Holmskjold, the man of parts – professor of natural history, politician, cabinet secretary to Queen Juliane Marie, director of the Copenhagen Botanical Garden and of the Royal Porcelain Manufactory – died in 1793. Though he was not to live to see the completion of the work, his part in its conception and in the first three years of actual work must have been considerable.

Mueller himself retired a year before the service was finally delivered to the Palace. By the end of November 1802 the new directors of the factory, Manthey and Grönland, were in correspondence with the General Post Office regarding the delivery of the service, in a somewhat obtuse effort to secure a speedy transfer of the valuable porcelain to the Moltke Palace[48] where the King resided after the fire at Christiansborg in 1794, and to obtain expeditious payment from the royal purse.

> We therefore have the honour to point out that in the books of the factory this service is assessed at 23,224 Rigsdaler, 3 Skilling and that only by receiving this sum will the factory be able to afford these expenses . . .

The letter went on:

> Moreover we think that we are entitled to ask that this service be taken off our hands as soon as possible because, being unique and perfect of its kind as a work of art, it cannot speedily enough be put to its destined use; and it may also be considered worthy to replace an older Sèvres service at the Royal table as evidence of the artistic diligence of our nation and to the glory of His Majesty who, by giving this commission, so graciously has stimulated our efforts. . . .

Another issue raised by the directors' communication to the Post Office, which requested that the matters contained therein should be referred to the Lord Chamberlain, was that of Bayer's future employment.

> Regarding painter Bayer we feel it incumbent upon us to add that his services hitherto have been employed partly in improving such pieces of the Flora Danica service as needed attention and partly in painting from nature; but as work of this kind is only very seldom needed and as he is handicapped by lack of practice, old age and weakness of vision, there is little more that he can do here at the factory.[49]

The Board of the General Post Office wrote to the Lord Chamberlain, Hauch, on 11 December 1802. It received a reply dated 19 January 1803:

> . . . it has pleased His Majesty, on my humble recommendation, most graciously to accept the Flora Danica service which has been offered; and His Majesty has furthermore entrusted me with the task of informing His Excellency, Privy Councillor Count Schimmelmann of this so that the latter may be able, through the Royal Treasury, to put the agreed sum at the disposition of His Majesty for settlement . . . although it may not be possible to reach a decision immediately about the money owing to the factory, I nevertheless have the honour to request that the service may be brought here, to the palace, at the beginning of next week and handed over to whoever may be appointed by me for the purpose of receiving it, so that it may be used here at Court on the occasion of His Majesty's exalted Birthday now approaching.

Bayer, who in 1801 had applied unsuccessfully for the post of painter-in-chief, was granted a pension equivalent to his annual salary in 1802. Two years later, at the age of 66, he left the factory for good. The full value of the service was never paid. In a letter to Schimmelmann, Hauch[50] quoted the King as saying that the factory could receive a capital sum of 10,000 Rixdollars in interest-bearing notes, payable over ten years. The balance of 13,224 Rd was written off the debt already incurred by the King. It was, to say the least, a one-sided financial arrangement.

Neither was the complete service delivered in time to greet the exalted Birthday. On 23 January 1803, Hauch wrote to the Post Office again, informing them that time was too short to permit the whole of the service to be delivered in time for the royal celebration. In any case there were no facilities immediately available for housing it. The Court Confectioner, who traditionally took charge of the Palace porcelain and table services, was instructed to receive those parts of the service used for dessert. Thus the Flora Danica pattern graced the dining table of Christian VII's Palace for the first time on Saturday 29 January 1803. It was some nine months later that the Lord Chamberlain returned to the question of finding a storage place for the entire service. On 19 September he wrote to the Commandant of the Rosenborg Palace asking if he had room for it. On 11 October Flora Danica was laid out on specially erected shelves in the Chinese Lacquered Room at the Rosenborg Palace.

The subsequent history of the service is one of wanton destruction, natural hazard and actual criminality, though for several decades it was to adorn the dining tables of the several royal palaces on the birthdays of successive monarchs, royal weddings, visits by foreign potentates and state occasions. After Christian VII's death in 1808, Frederik VI continued to occupy the Schack Palace, using the Moltke Palace only for official purposes. Stately processions filed from one establishment to another for the great banquets of the time, and at the most important of them Flora Danica was set amid the splendour of the Louis Seize interior designed by N.-H. Jardin at the Moltke Palace within the Amalienborg complex. Its gilded ornamentation sparkling in the light of a hundred candles and the reflections of the chandeliers must have presented a breathtaking spectacle. But the kings of eighteenth-century and early nineteenth-century Europe were no great respectors of the arts and crafts lavished on them by loyal and obedient subjects. It is estimated that on average one piece of the Flora Danica service was lost with every banquet at which it was used. The fine basketry work of the pieces used mainly for desserts was especially vulnerable to the assaults of hosts and their guests. Extracts from the diaries of Johan Bülow, Lord Chamberlain to Frederik VI before his accession, give some idea of the dangers to which the proudest achievement of the Mueller factory was prone. Of a hunting luncheon in 1810 he wrote:

> When the hunting ardour of the gallant Nimrods had been cooled by the blood of the animals they had killed, and their failing powers had been restored by a delicate collation in which the gifts of Bacchus played a prominent part, they began as usual to pelt one another with bread and bones. Potatoes were here used with extraordinary effect. The King armed himself with an enormously powerful weapon – some plates of stewed fruit to wit – and with these the battle was won. They flew around like cannon balls, with great accuracy, nearly always hitting the target, and one can well imagine what effect the custard had on faces and clothes when this splendid joke was over.

In the reign of Frederik VI's successor,

> Tortoise soup with fish balls or soup à la Brunnaise with croquettes
> Small Cromequis with mushrooms
> Salmon au bleu with potatoes and 2 kinds of sauce
> Game à la broche with jelly and 2 sauces or lamb à la broche with spinach and pickles
> Asparagus and Randers salmon or green peas and breast of goose
> Partridge à l'espagnole
> Vol au vent with Jerusalem artichokes
> Ice pudding à la Celestine
> Roast pheasants with salad and compote
> Strassburg liver paste with truffles
> Cake
> 3 kinds of ices with biscuits and meringues
> Dessert
>
> Leoville
> Port or Madeira
> St. Peray
> Chateau Latour
> Rosenborg white wine
> Red and white Champagne
> Cap Constantia

31 *Menu for New Year banquet at Amalienborg Palace during reign of Christian VIII, at which Flora Danica service was used.*

Christian VIII (1839-48), the service was in frequent use and much of it was broken. In one dinner-time extravaganza 32 plates were smashed or otherwise damaged.

In 1828 the Christiansborg Palace was restored and again became the residence of the reigning monarch. Part of the Flora Danica service was transferred to it along with many other valuable articles from Amalienborg. The new royal palace was to prove no safer as a repository than its predecessor, however. On the night of 3 October 1884 another fire at Christiansborg caused yet further destruction of Denmark's art treasures, and another 43 pieces[51] of Flora Danica were lost. The rest of the service was hastily removed to the royal chapel with sparks raining down on the rescuers. The fire spread rapidly and eventually the chapel was threatened and the porcelain, along with the royal silver, was transferred back to Amalienborg. Many of the engraved plates for the service, also housed with the royal collection, were destroyed in the fire.

In fact, only about two hundred pieces of Flora Danica were at Christiansborg at the time of the second fire, recalled from the keeping of the Superintendent of Rosenborg, in whose care the service had been placed in 1851. The order of the Lord Chamberlain's office to Superintendent Stouenberg, dated 27 November 1851, specified that it should be

[51] A. G. Hassø, *Christiansborg Brand*, Copenhagen, 1934. See Grandjean, *op.cit.*, note 42; in 1885, 43 new pieces were ordered, several of the replacements were copied from sherds.

ROYAL COPENHAGEN

'incorporated in the inventories of Rosenborg Palace', but as late as 1862 the director of Rosenborg complained that the order had not been carried out.[52]

In 1862-63 the Palace director apportioned the collection between Rosenborg and the Statsinventariekommissionen of the Danish Home Office. Charles XV, King of Sweden and connoisseur of porcelain, arrived at Copenhagen in 1862 and greatly admired the Flora Danica. He was presented with a flower basket and a dessert dish[53] by Frederik VII.

Two years before, the King had presented another basket with modelled flowers to the English visitor Sir Horace Marryat, whose own book, *A History of Pottery and Porcelain*,[54] records that it was in the loan collection of the Victoria and Albert Museum from 1868. The basket remained in the loan collection until its donor's death in 1888, when it was returned to the family. It has not since been traced.[55]

These are the only pieces known to have been given away by the service's royal owners. But many others disappeared. It was not until 1906 that the full extent of the losses or their cause became known. On 1 March of that year the journal *Vort Land* contained an article by Prof. Arnold Krog, Art Director of the Royal Manufactory, openly accusing a keeper of the Rosenborg collection of having sold illegally pieces from the service. Krog, who knew the royal service intimately, had seen pieces in several antique shops and on inquiry had been told that the keeper had sold them. He demanded an investigation into the matter. The keeper attempted to defend himself by sueing Krog, but withdrew his case at the first hearing and afterwards admitted that in two years he had disposed of 101 pieces of Flora Danica and many other objects from the chronological Rosenborg collection. Eighty-one pieces were returned to the collection, and twenty disappeared abroad, never to be recovered. Five of the returned pieces were from museums overseas which had purchased them in good faith. When the legal proceedings were over they were returned to the museums which had bought them. Of the twenty pieces that were never traced, four are known to have been sold at a Budapest auction. Two plates were retained (by permission) by the Berlin Schlossmuseum, marked *Ceraftium alpinum VI, Fasc.1*, and *Fucus digitatus CCCXCII, Fasc.7*. Both were lost with the rest of the museum's porcelain in World War II. An ice box with casserole and lid and one shell dish were similarly retained by the Hamburg Museum für Kunst und Gewerbe.[56]

Not a single piece of the Flora Danica pattern was made for 60 years after the delivery of the royal service in 1803, even for replacement purposes. In the autumn of 1862, however, Princess Alexandra, daughter of Christian IX, was betrothed to Britain's Prince of Wales, later Edward VII. A committee of ladies formed in Denmark with the object of presenting a suitable wedding present to the royal couple decided that a new Flora Danica service should be commissioned. Although the wedding took place on 10 March 1863, the service was not completed until February 1864.

The Princess Alexandra service[57] consists of 725 pieces and was intended for 60 people. The strictly botanical nature of the illustrations on the original service was jettisoned; it has been said that they found little favour 'in the critical eyes of this committee of ladies'. New volumes of the book *Flora Danica* had appeared since 1799, and different plants were chosen for the new porcelain work. On the dessert pieces, views of Danish castles and mansions were used, and in some cases more colourful renderings of plants from the Botanical Gardens of Copenhagen took the place of book illustrations.[58]

The new service caused a revival of the old pearl shape that was the foundation stone of Flora Danica, and a number of services decorated with the flowers of Denmark were made in the ensuing 20 years at the Kobmager Street factory. In 1884 the factory moved to its present-day site in Frederiksborg. From then until the present Flora Danica has been produced without interruption, though in relatively small quantity, from the original hand-coloured engravings. But the porcelain decoration has changed with the differing tastes and techniques of succeeding generations. Chromatic colours, first used on the Princess Alexandra service, have replaced the more sombre rust colours of the original service. Some of the detail of the old botanical illustrations has given way to a more free-hand manner of painting. Old disciplines have given way to new aesthetic values. But the basic constraint remains: fidelity to the plant life of Denmark and (until 1814) of the dual kingdom of Norway.[59]

Early pieces all contained a legend on the undersides of flatware and dishes, the number of the engraving from which they originated and the part number of the botanical work. Nowadays only the Latin name of the plant is written on the base, in black script. An excep-

---

[52] Letter from director, J. J. A. Worsaae, to Rosenborg administration, 15 June 1862. Grandjean, *op.cit.*, note 38.

[53] Now in National Museum, Stockholm.

[54] London, 1868, p.361.

[55] W. B. Honey (formerly head of Ceramics Department, V & A) to B. L. Grandjean, *op.cit.*, p.80.

[56] Dr Martin Klar, Berlin, to B. L. Grandjean, *op.cit.*, p.80.

[57] Originally at Sandringham, since removed to state apartments, Windsor Castle.

[58] Johan Lange to F. E. Holm, factory director, factory archive. Grandjean, *op.cit.*, note 44.

[59] Loss of Norway, treaty of Kiel, 1814. Great national distress and constitutional agitation followed, 1815-30.

tion is provided by the Flora Danica pieces decorated by Arnold Krog after 1905 in an attempt to recreate the pieces of the first royal service. These were marked with a new factory emblem known as the 'Queen Juliane Marie' mark with crown superior.

A number of pearl designs have been added to the factory's range since 1862, but essentially the relief-bordered wares of the late eighteenth century remain the basis of Flora Danica porcelain in the twentieth century.

Of the 1,802 pieces of the original service delivered in 1803, 1,530 survive to the present day in the Porcelain Room of Rosenborg, and in the Turret Room by the Knight's Hall of the ancient palace. With its rustic colouring, based on copper enamels, and its strict adherence to the botanical illustrations which are its *raison d'être*, it is not everyone's favourite example of ceramic art, either among the many offerings of the Royal Copenhagen Manufactory or among those of the European porcelain factories in general. But for many it is one of the greatest achievements of European decorative art. The German art historian Fr. H. Hofmann in his *Das Porzellan der Europaischen Manufakturen im 18. Jahrhundert*,[60] brackets Flora Danica with the Swan Service for Count Bruehl begun at Meissen in 1737 from Kaendler's drawings. That is praise enough.

[60] Publ. 1932

Note: Adherence to engravings in *Flora Danica*. The Danish art historian Victor P. Christensen declared in a monograph (Den Kgl. Danske Porcelainfabrik i 18, 1938) that 'the service and the book have nothing in common beyond their name'. That is patently untrue, as testified by many expert judges, by simple comparison and by visitors to the factory at the time of its execution. See Grandjean, *op.cit.*, pp. 46-48.

32 *Pieces from the Queen Alexandra Flora Danica service commissioned by a 'Committee of Ladies' of Denmark on the engagement of the Princess to Edward VII in 1862, delivered in 1864, a year after the wedding. Now in the state apartments, Windsor. Picture by gracious permission of HM the Queen. Copyright reserved.*

ROYAL COPENHAGEN

33 Tureen and cover from Flora Danica service, twentieth century. Each piece is decorated entirely by hand; fidelity to the original drawings and to plant life remains the guiding rule.

34 Ice-bell, from a present-day Flora Danica service.

FLORA DANICA

34

35 *Entwined plants, moulded flowers and immaculate gilding, on a present-day Flora Danica tureen.*

36 *Plate, cup and saucer and serving dish from present-day Flora Danica service.*

36

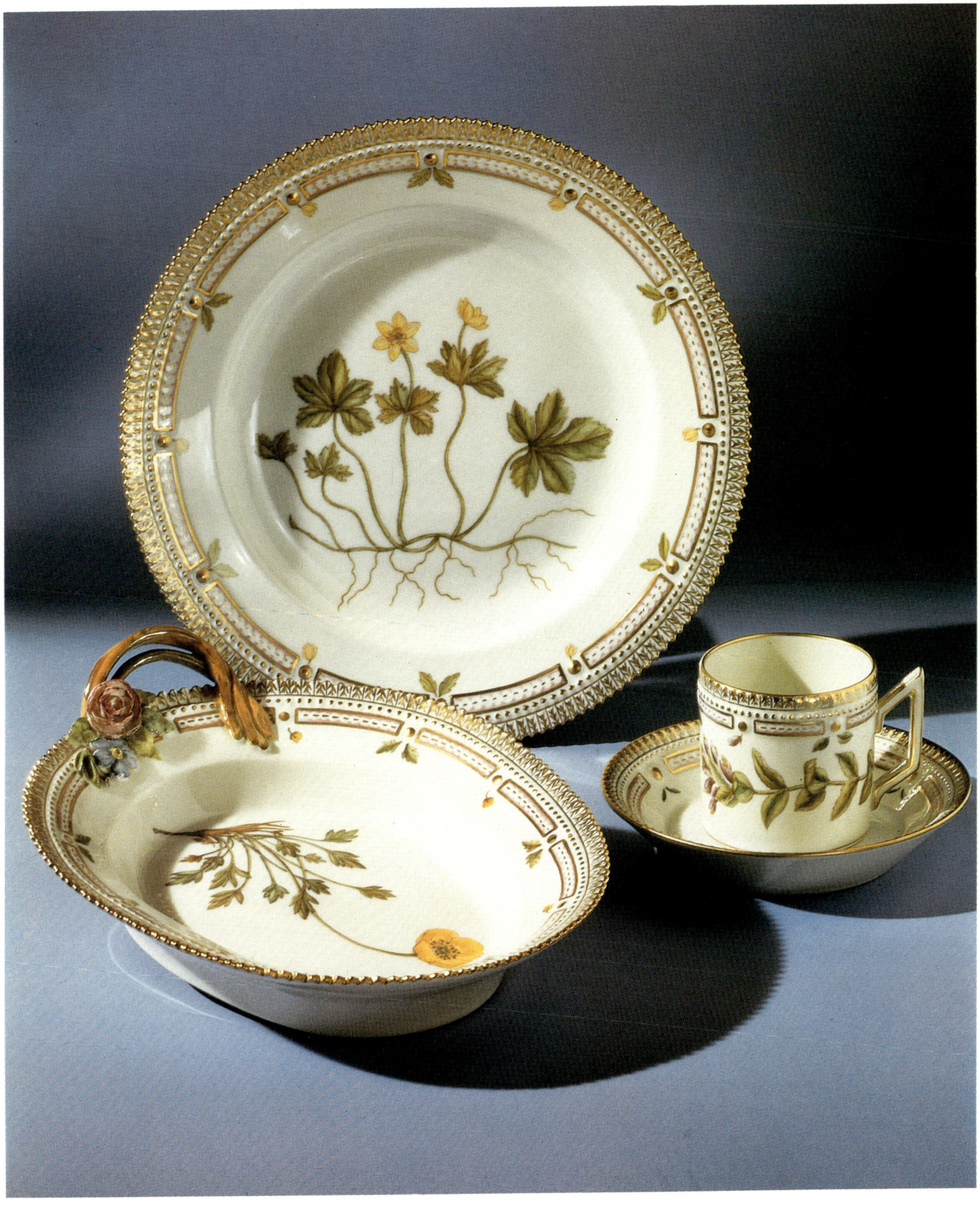

ROYAL COPENHAGEN

6
Blue and White

IF Flora Danica is seen by many observers as the high-point of decorative achievement at the Royal Manufactory of Denmark, others regard its mastery of painting in underglaze blue as the most pervasive triumph.

Copenhagen, like other European potteries working in earthenware and porcelainous clays for some two centuries before its birth, looked most covetously at the blue-decorated wares of the Orient. Royal Copenhagen was to seek its inspiration from the designs through which the masters of Saxony had transmuted Chinese patterns into the more restrained, stylised manner of European ceramic art; and the Danish factory was to prove lavish in its own contribution to the most common, yet in many ways the most exacting, of all forms of decoration. Designs which could be traced from the earliest porcelain of Saxony through the delft and maiolica earthenwares of Italy, England and Holland back to the Yüan dynasty of China in the thirteenth and fourteenth centuries, took on renewed vitality at Copenhagen; to such an extent that a design which was essentially derivative of other factories became known to the world as the 'Copenhagen' pattern.

Cobalt is the essential ingredient of blue

37 *Blue Flowers and Blue-Fluted. Dinner plates from the Mueller factory, c. 1780, each measuring 10in (254mm). Royal Copenhagen Museum.*

decoration, found as an oxide ore in several parts of the world. It was first used by the potters of Mesopotamia in the ninth century on an opaque tin glaze,[61] a technique later used in maiolica and Dutch and English delftwares. A little later the Chinese potters of the Golden Age of the T'ang emperors began to employ a splash decorating technique using cobalt in the glaze; occasionally these blue glazes were used to fill in incised or stamped designs.[62]

The technique of painting with cobalt oxide under the glaze was probably first used by the Kashan potters of Persia in the thirteenth century, the pigment being applied directly to the dried body on wares with a marked similarity to European soft-paste porcelain.[63]

The Kashan wares were probably made in imitation of the Ting and *ying ch'ing* Sung porcelains[64] of China, both of which were exported to the Near East, with their carved decoration. But the Persian blue, though giving a fine colour, was liable to run, as the Chinese were to discover when they tried to use Kashan cobalt. It had to be used in broad painted bands or superimposed on outlines of a more tractable black pigment.[65]

Early Chinese blue and white underglaze wares of the late thirteenth century developed out of the techniques already established in using copper oxide pigments, fired in a reducing atmosphere to give reds of many hues. Difficulties and failures in the use of copper under the glaze had taught the Chinese valuable lessons. The blue wares, which made a tentative appearance in the late Yüan period and which flowered into the very highest manifestation of ceramic art in the Ming dynasty, were uniquely attractive to western eyes; and rightly so, for they are unique. Western potters would aspire to the best of them, learning and then forgetting the techniques of underglaze decoration, emulating their colouring effects and seeking inspiration in their flowing lines, the assured adaptation of natural motifs into abstract patterns of incredible beauty. In a few cases they would approach the finest of the Ming and Ch'ing wares, though in truth they would never equal them.

In his prospectus for a Danish porcelain factory of 1774, Frantz Henrich Mueller mentioned that he had made careful study of the use of colours, 'especially the blue, so-called ultramarine colour which the Chinese use for their blue and white porcelain'. From the outset, great importance was attached by the factory to the production of good underglaze decorated wares which would withstand constant use, be reasonably priced (though by no means within the means of the mass of the population), and admirable in appearance. Such wares would require only two firings.[66] In 1776 the board of directors instructed that 'no other colour than the blue should be employed for the decoration of the porcelain'. In 1778 eight out of every ten painters worked exclusively with cobalt blue.[67]

Mussel-painted or Blue Fluted

The blue-painted wares of Ming China presented an irresistible challenge to the potters of Europe long before the advent of hard-paste porcelain manufacture at the beginning of the eighteenth century.

It was the mastery of the 'true' porcelain, however, with its feldspathic glazes which enabled blue decoration (and copper browns and greens for that matter) to be painted under the glaze and fused in the high glost fire, that gave rise to large-scale emulation in Europe of the charismatic Oriental wares. Meissen, inevitably, was the first factory to produce an artistically and commercially acceptable design which echoed the themes of entwined flower stems and floral blooms delicately drawn in outline, or harmoniously arranged in luscious blobs of blue, which recurred during the previous five centuries of Chinese ceramic art. In fact, in its first thirty years the Dresden factory produced two notable designs in underglaze blue, one of them described as 'Blau gerippt oder glatt' (blue, fluted or plain), the other 'Zwiebelmuster' ('onion pattern'). They were quickly copied by other factories, notably those of Thuringia. The potteries of Switzerland, Holland, France, Denmark and England also chose to follow suit.

The early eighteenth-century potters were, of course, familiar with blue-painted renderings of Oriental themes in delftware and soft-paste porcelains[68] which, since about 1650, had become the vehicles for westernised versions of Chinese decorative motifs, *chinoiserie*, assimilated and invested with Occidental ideas and artistic traits. English potters would contribute a famous example in earthenware, and later in bone china, the so-called 'Willow Pattern'.[69]

But blue-and-white was the everyday ware of Europe, the poor man's platter to be used for eating purposes rather than to be admired in the closed cabinet, whereas in China it had been established for centuries as the 'classic'

[61] The tin oxide was added to the lead glaze.

[62] See Garner, Sir Harry, *Oriental Blue and White*, Faber, 1954. T'ang dynasty 618-906. Blue-glaze decoration towards end of period; quotes Trans. of Oriental Ceramic Society, 1935-6, H. C. Gallois, About T'ang and Ta Ts'in.

[63] See Lane, Arthur, *Early Islamic Pottery*, Faber, 1957, p.6 *et seq*.

[64] *ibid*.

[65] Garner, *op.cit.*. Chemical analysis suggests that the earliest T'ang blue glaze wares were coloured with imported Persian cobalt, known as 'Mohammadan blue' p.3-5. 'The Mohammadan blue by itself tended to run and . . . was mixed with the native (Chinese) ore to give firm outlines', p.16.

[66] Chinese blue painted wares were fired once only, in the glost kiln.

[67] Grandjean, *Blaablomstrede Stel*. Factory monograph, 1968.

[68] Underglaze blue decoration on Medici soft-paste 1575-87, e.g. pieces from Fitzhenry Collection, V & A Museum.

[69] See Watney, Bernard, *English Blue and White Porcelain of the 18th Century*, Faber, 1963, Introduction. Willow pattern, attrib. to Thomas Minton at Caughley, c.1775-80.

ROYAL COPENHAGEN

[70] From about 1683 when the imperial kilns were reorganised, overglaze enamels came into official favour, with the *famille verte* and *famille rose*, and these wares exerted considerable influence on European taste.

[71] Grandjean, *Det Musselmalede Stel*, Factory monograph, Copenhagen, 1950, p.12.

[72] Hannover, Emil, *Keramisk Haandbog*, vol.II, 2 (1924), quoted by Grandjean, *ibid*.

ware.[70] The absence of pretentiousness was to prove its great strength.

In his history of the Meissen factory Karl Berling does not even mention the Mussel pattern, or 'Muschel' as the Germans called it. Indeed, the factory took it out of production a few years after its inception, probably irritated by copyists, and the 'Onion' pattern became the typical blue-and-white decoration of the Saxony potters.

Nevertheless, the rich Meissen pattern, based on the *Strohblume*, the little blue flower known in England as the *immortelle* or wild aster, was the primogenitor of all that followed. Karl Berling,[71] in a bicentenary jubilee publication of 1910, cited a reference to 'the fluted design' in the files of the Royal (Saxony) Household, dated 1736. Emil Hannover, the Danish art historian, believed that he had traced the first Meissen version to 'about 1740'.[72] No more exact date than this can be arrived at.

Berling also wrote: 'When this unobtrusive pattern . . . appears for the first time, is indeed difficult to say. I believe I have found it in the price list of 1765.' But that would seem to be

38 and 39 *Half and full lace versions of the Blue-Fluted pattern, introduced c. 1776 and revived by Arnold Krog between 1885 and 1895. Still in production.*

BLUE AND WHITE

39

ROYAL COPENHAGEN

40 *Dish, c. 1785, exhibiting characteristic blue-grey appearance of decoration under greyish glaze resulting from impurities in the clay and firing problems. When discolouration was complete, deformities were sometimes corrected by green painting over the glaze. Royal Copenhagen Museum.*

[73] See Watney, *op.cit.*, p.52.

[74] Grandjean, *Det Musselmalede Stel*, Factory monograph, Copenhagen, 1950.

[75] Grandjean, *op.cit.*, p.12.

too late. Between 1760 and 1783, the 'immortelle' pattern found its way on to Worcester soft-paste and a little later on Caughley, Lowestoft and New Hall wares, and was often referred to as the 'Copenhagen' pattern.[73] According to Hannover the pattern was introduced at Copenhagen by Luplau in 1776. He offers no evidence, but there is no reason to doubt his assertion. There is much more reason to doubt his and other explanations of the term 'musselmalet': mussel-painted.

Arnold Krog, who in the late nineteenth century was to become the Royal Manufactory's most dynamic and distinguished art director, wrote of the Mussel pattern:

> The origin of the word mussel is obscure. Supposedly the term originates from the fact that the pattern was painted with blue cobalt pigment, known of old as mussel colour. The same colour was used by the Chinese who imported it from Persia by Muhammadans (Musselmans). The word 'mussel' or 'musel' is hence supposed to be derived from the place-name Mosul.

The modern historian Bredo L. Grandjean has dealt with three hypotheses in an extensively researched paper[74] on the subject: that 'mussel' refers to (1) the shape on which it is painted, (2) the colour used and (3) the motif itself.

The terms used by various factories to describe the service are cited.

Meissen, 1765: 'Blau gerippt oder glatt'. Blue fluted or plain.
Ilmenau, 1787: 'Blau gerieft Meissner Modell'. Blue fluted, Meissen model.
Amstel, 1798: 'Cobold blauw geriht Sax. patroon'. Cobalt blue fluted Saxon pattern.
Nyon, 1800: 'Decor en bleu et blanc façon de Saxe'. Decoration in blue and white Saxon shape.
Rörstrand, 1874: 'Sachsiskt monster'. Saxon pattern.
Royal Copenhagen, 1893: (English price list) 'blue fluted'.

The oldest surviving reference in a Copenhagen factory price list (1779) reads: 'rifl. blaat og hvidt saxisk Tegning'. There is also reference to 'ordinaer glat' and 'ordinaer riflet'. Thus, Fluted blue and white Saxon design – ordinary plain, ordinary fluted. In 1793, we have 'Saxisk Mønster Muselmodel', Saxon pattern Mussel model.

The word 'mussel' is shown in the Concise Danish Dictionary to derive from 'musling' (shellfish, mussel). 'Yet another example of nature having inspired the craftsman', suggests Grandjean. There is, however, a close connection between 'mussel' and the German 'Muschel' (muscle). And there is an etymological connection in English, the name of the shellfish having the same Latin derivation as the anatomical word (*musculum*, nom.). Hannover uses the terms 'Mussel', 'Muschel' and 'Mume' (the latter strictly referring to the oriental peach tree *Prunus Mume*) interchangeably. He also translates 'mume-flower' as *Strohblume*, which is the same plant as the English *immortelle* flower. But the German *Muschelblume*, the only plant which could be related to the term 'mussel', is a floating water plant, *Pistia stratiotes*, which has no likeness to the flowers of the porcelain pattern.[75] As for the idea that 'mussel' refers to the blue colour, deriving from Musselman (or mussel) blue, Grandjean points to a red mussel service mentioned in the Copenhagen auction catalogue for the year 1796 when, at Mueller's instigation, much of the company's porcelain stock was sold off to repair its ailing finances. The Zurich factory also made a red service in the 'mussel' pattern. Thus, the accepted view is that the name refers to the shape of the pieces in the service, however tenuous the visual connection may be between the fluted design and the mussel shell.

But there is another factor which could explain the Danish origin of the name, and one which has been ignored by Danish and other historians. In 1772, three years before the foundation of the factory in Kobmagergade, Denmark became the world centre of Islamic interest and scholarship with the publication of Carsten Niebuhr's book *Beschreibung von Arabien* in Copenhagen. It is difficult to reconstruct at a remove of two centuries the sensation caused by the return of the young German who had become an adopted Dane on 20 November 1767, the only survivor of an expedition of six quarrelsome men who had departed Denmark seven years earlier at the instigation of Frederik V to make a scientific survey of Arabia. Niebuhr's bravery and diligent scholarship were to give him a unique place among explorers of the desert lands of the Near East. When Gibbon came to write his *History of the Decline and Fall of the Roman Empire*, he relied for his description of the Arabs and the 'Musselmans' in his famous Fiftieth Chapter on Niebuhr's book and his subsequently published diaries and notes. Of Arabia Felix, so minutely described by Niebuhr: 'It was for this earthly paradise that Nature had reserved her choicest favours and her most curious workmanship: the incompatible blessings of luxury and innocence were ascribed to the natives: the soil was impregnated with gold and gems . . . '.[76] The most significant aspect of the explorer's tragic journey and his description of the Islamic heartland, however, was its awakening of a scholarly interest in the workmanship, the pottery and metalcraft, manuscript illumination and so forth of Mesopotamia, Syria and the other lands through which he travelled. The early eighteenth-century letters from China of Père d'Entrecolles the Jesuit missionary, and the observations of other travellers who had described the potters of Persia and Mesopotamia at work, took on a new importance. Musselmans and the Musselman or Muhammadan Blue were on the tips of many tongues in Denmark in the late eighteenth century. The descriptions by d'Entrecolles of the Chinese kilns and the Muhammadan Blue,[77] written between 1712 and 1722, give some idea of the fascination of the subject to western potters:

> A beautiful blue colour appears on porcelain after having been lost for some time. When the colour is first painted on, it is pale black; when it is dry and the glaze has been put on it, it disappears entirely and the porcelain seems quite white, the colour being buried under the glaze. But the fire makes it appear in all its beauty, almost in the same way as the natural heat of the sun makes the most beautiful butterflies, with all their tints, come out of their eggs.

It seems possible, at least, that the familiar term 'Musselman' (deriving from Muslim not Mosel[78]) was declined to 'Mussel' in Danish usage when applied to the blue colour, and that having become accepted it was applied to the pattern itself. In any event, the etymology of the word is unimportant. Whatever their origins, the names 'Mussel-Painted', 'Mussel-Model' and 'Blue Fluted' can hardly be regarded as inspired nomenclature. The epithet 'Immortelle' applied to the tiny flower which is its dominant theme is altogether more attractive and meaningful. 'Copenhagen' is the name by which the world has come to

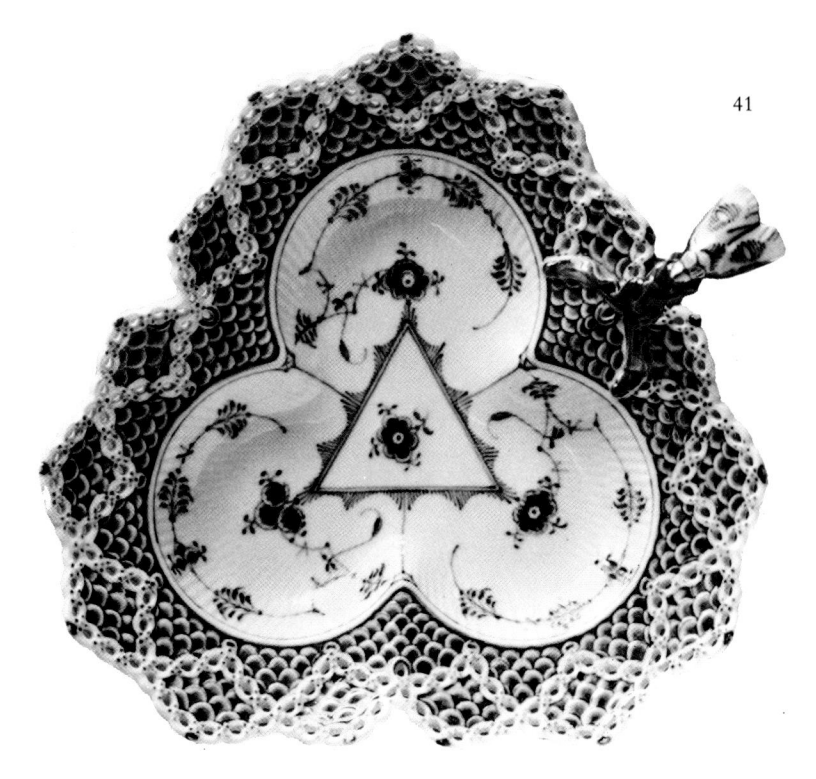

41 *Tray using reduced and simplified version of the Immortelle theme – with single and triple 'blooms' – and interacting circular and triangular shapes. Heavily laced border, 'insect' handle. Designed by Krog, 1887. Dimensions 10 × 8in (250 × 200mm). Royal Copenhagen Museum.*

[76] See essay, 'Carsten Niebuhr, Survivor of a Tragic Expedition', in *Explorers of Arabia* by Freeth and Winstone, Allen & Unwin, 1978. Also *Arabien: Dokumente zur Entdeckungs-geschichte, Niebuhrs Reise in den Yemen*, Stuttgart, 1965.

[77] According to Ming annals, fourteenth and fifteenth centuries, *hui hui ch'ing* (Muhammadan Blue) among other articles of tribute arrived in China. See Garner, *Oriental Blue and White*, p.15, and *T'ang Shi Szu K'ao*, published 1778. (See Bushell, S. W., *Description of Chinese Pottery and Porcelain*, being a translation of the *T'ao Shuo*, Oxford, 1910, for general appraisal of Chinese methods and attitudes.)

[78] Maslam (Muslim), past participle of Aslama, 'at peace', hence Islam.

42

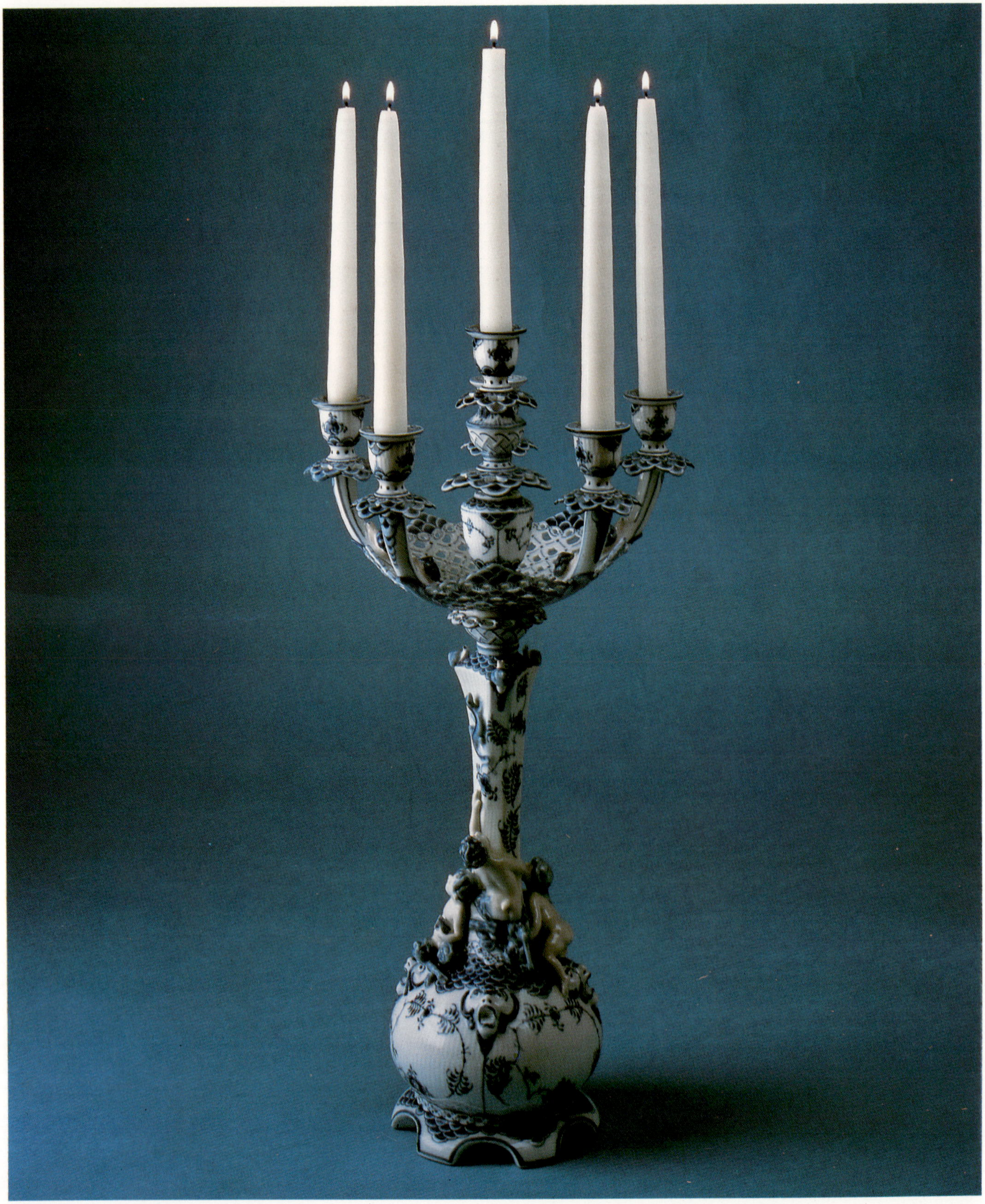

BLUE AND WHITE

know the pattern.

By the time Mueller's factory began to decorate both fluted and plain wares with the *Strohblume* or *Blaublümchen* of the German version, earthenware factories in Denmark had already taken it up. But the Danish version differed from Meissen's in essential respects. Two rings instead of one were painted in the middle of plates. The flowers were closely copied from Meissen but in other respects the abstract pattern derives more from the Thuringian versions. Soon after the inception of the design at Copenhagen, c.1776, two more luxurious versions appeared, half- and full-lace services, with closed and open lacework respectively on plates and dishes. This was a Danish innovation. Other variations on this Chinese-inspired decoration appeared at the same time, generally following the Meissen examples – 'Onion', 'Star' pattern, festoons, 'Blue Flowers'. From 1800, however, only the Mussel service and Blue Flowers remained in the Royal Manufactory's range. Other earthenware factories of the early nineteenth century copied the popular pattern; Oland (1804-1840) and Antvorskov (1811-1815), for example. Mussel-painted services had already become part of the Danish national heritage. It was to become over the following years the most popular and by far the most widely copied of all porcelain and china services in the western world. Even such items as writing sets and flower pots were decorated with the pattern.

In 1853 another porcelain factory was established in Copenhagen, Bing and Grondahl. It was to exist alongside the royal factory in friendly but intense rivalry, each gaining artistic and technical sustenance from the other as the years went by, chiefly through the interchange of key craftsmen and designers but often through a shared response to the *Zeitgeist*. There are examples of sheer plagiarism too, though in the terms of the ceramic industry, which is essentially derivative, the word should not be regarded as emotive or admonitory. In 1875 Bing and Grondahl began to produce a Mussel-painted service, although this differed from the Royal Copenhagen version in its outline flowers: the latter filled the tiny flowers with colour. At the end of the nineteenth century the painter F. A. Hallin designed for Bing and Grondahl a new version based on a scale pattern and divided into three segments instead of the customary four. At about the same time that factory produced a design known as 'Butterfly', painted on Hallin's scale pattern. The Danish earthenware factory Aluminia, founded in 1863 and later (1884) amalgamated with the Royal Manufactory, adopted the pattern from 1868, painted on fluted and plain wares. It also produced a simplified version, similar to that of the Swedish factory Gustavsberg, which had adopted a mussel decoration in the latter part of the eighteenth century. Among other factories to follow suit were Furnivals of Staffordshire, Rörstrand, Porsgrund of Norway, Gladding and McBean (Fransiscan) of Los Angeles and Enoch Wedgwood.

42 *Candelabrum decorated with cleverly adapted 'Immortelle' pattern and lace work. Designed by Krog, 1885. Still in production.*

43 *Pieces from nineteenth century with characteristic Copenhagen double circle on plates, and coffee pot exhibiting imaginative alliance of Immortelle elements with curved and straight planes. Pierced edges. Still in production.*

ROYAL COPENHAGEN

44 *Full-lace Blue-Fluted service designed by Krog, c. 1885-95. In current production.*

45 *Early Copenhagen blue painting on ink-stand, discoloured under greyish semi-matt glaze. Painter's mark X (unidentified); thrower's mark large inscribed K and triangle. Date 1775-79. Height 3½in (85mm). Royal Copenhagen Museum.*

It was the later art director of Royal Copenhagen, Arnold Krog, who found in the 'Mussel' pattern initial inspiration and who finally made it into a byword of ceramic art, synonymous with 'Copenhagen': a design for all time. After joining the factory in 1885, he wrote:

> One of the first days I found a mussel-painted plate – one from the old days. I looked at its beautiful, bright surface (it was not fluted), its delightful, somewhat grey-green brightness and its dreamlike indigo blue colour . . . It was this precious plate which opened my eyes to a new world from which I took my little part.

There is an implied criticism of contemporary work in Krog's praise of the old plate. Indeed, the standard of workmanship and artistry had declined noticeably in the nineteenth century, as at most other factories, as the industrial revolution gained strength and hand began to give way to machine. Krog came at the moment of revival, as the arts and crafts movement born in England began to fight back. From one plate he was to create an entirely new service with broad richly perforated lace borders and luxurious colour decoration. The factory's chemist in Krog's time, Clément, improved both glaze and pigment. In an ironic cycle of imitation, the German factories reintroduced the mussel pattern as 'Kopenhagen Muster'. In 1925-30 in a court action brought in the Landsretten (High Court), which was referred to the Hojesteret (Supreme Court), it was held that the copyright of the models themselves belonged to the factory, but that the mussel pattern was common property. Another artist of the late nineteenth century made important contributions to the rejuvenation of the design. He was Oluf Jensen who was apprenticed to the decorating workshop in 1885, and some of whose pieces are indistinguishable from their eighteenth-century counterparts. By 1910, three versions of the Blue Fluted service, with plain edges, half-lace and full-lace, comprised more than 1,500 items.

Blue Flowers
Handwritten price lists sent by C. J. C. Klipfel, the leading painter and later director of the Berlin factory, to Mueller in 1779 referred to services 'mit deutschen Blumen'. In 1780 'Danish Blue Flowers' appeared in the Copenhagen lists. The 'Danish' designation was quickly abandoned, and from the early 1780s to the present day 'Blue Flowers' were to occupy an honoured place in the range of

the Royal Manufactory. Though there have been slight stylistic changes in the handpainting of these boldly drawn flowers, the essential techniques have remained unchanged.

Problems of blue decoration encountered by Mueller in the first twenty years[79] or so are underlined by surviving records relating to Blue Flowers in particular. It was found in the early stages that the feldspathic glaze applied to the decorated bisque intensified the blue during the second firing. The cobalt ore used at that time came from Modum in Norway, and it was found to be less pure than the German ore (from Saxony). Iron and other mineral impurities had to be removed thoroughly. There was also the problem of carbon-infested smoke in the kiln discolouring the surface.[80]

Production of wares bearing the names of the famous German basketwork patterns, such as 'Alt Ozier' (1735), 'Alt Brandenstein' (1738), 'Neu Brandenstein' (1744) and 'Neu Ozier' (1745), began in 1775 at Copenhagen. Few pieces from this early period survive, and those which can be seen at the present day confirm their reliance on the Meissen examples, with curved shapes in the rococo style. They generally bore their original German names, or slight variations, such as 'Fluted Ozier' and 'Curved Shape'. Most of the surviving pieces also exemplify the early technical difficulties. An intended clear blue under a pure glaze became a grey-blue under a yellowish, grey-green or grey-blue glaze. Usually such kiln disasters were concealed by the application of clever on-glaze green decoration. Such attentions, of course, demanded a third firing in the decorating kiln and could not have been financially profitable. However, one painter, Abraham Schlegel,[81] is known to have been retained to make such repairs.

The Danish version of 'Alt Ozier' was decorated on the glaze, and the same is true of a version of about 1780 painted only on tea and coffee sets. The Copenhagen relief decoration and simulated basketwork is simply interrupted, while in the German design it is actually sectioned. A few examples of Brandenstein-type decoration exist in the older pattern, but the Danish name for them is unrecorded. During the early Mueller period, 1775-80, Blue Flowers were painted on 'medallion' panels (fig.47) on various plain shapes, and on vases, ink-stands and flower and chamber pots, with and without lids. The pearl pattern, primarily used for Flora Danica decoration, was occasionally used for Blue

46 *Water bottle with girdle entwined with small leaves, blue flowers under a yellowish matt glaze with a porous constitution. Painter's mark, two parallel lines, possibly Lars Hansen; thrower's mark 4 and triangle. Collar chipped. Before 1779. Height 9in (230mm). Private collection.*

47 *Pair of custard cups with pale blue decoration on the 'medallion' pattern. Painter's mark K, c. 1780. Height 3in (80mm). Royal Copenhagen Museum.*

[79]The factory's chemist from 1782 to 1796, Johan Koren Blyt, was engaged in experiments which were responsible for the exceptional quality of the Copenhagen blue in the Mueller period.

[80]See Grandjean, *Blaablomestrede Stel*, Factory monograph, Copenhagen, 1968.

[81]Schlegel 1780 in records, but possibly at factory before that date.

48 *Oval tureen with deep blue decoration. Painter's mark 2, c. 1790. Overall length 15in (380mm). Royal Copenhagen Museum.*

Flowers. Up to 1799 Mueller used three body clay formulae, one of which (known as No.II) had a very high percentage of Bornholm kaolin and only about 15 per cent of feldspar and silica. Its fluxing quality would have been far too low to permit its use other than for special purposes, perhaps items such as casseroles and other large or elaborate pieces. Generally, up to 1793, No.I clay was used, with some 54 per cent quartz and 37 per cent Bornholm kaolin, giving a grey colour which was often speckled under a thick glossy glaze. From that date a mix containing more than 40 per cent of French kaolin and only about 12 per cent Bornholm clay was employed. It gave a much whiter body and had many other desirable qualities such as plasticity in handling, and great strength when fired. The 'virgin' mix, containing no silica and a preponderance of French kaolin, was used for the pearl shapes and other enamel decorated wares from 1779.

But if the improved clays were to give the blue-painted wares a wider commercial acceptability, it was the duller greyish Bornholm body of the early years, giving a hazy almost dreamlike quality to the blue flowers under a thick glaze, which attracted Krog; and have always attracted the connoisseur. Painting on the early pieces is thinly drawn and meticulous, bearing the stamp of on-glaze decorators accustomed to working from copper-engraved originals. From 1780 trained 'blue' painters appeared on the scene, alternating between the Blue-Fluted and Blue Flower patterns,[82] and working on other rare items of the time such as the 'Indian' version of Meissen's 'Fels und Vogel' and a similar Fürstenberg design, and the Onion and Star patterns. Since the foundations of the factory every blue piece has been given the mark of each journeyman or painter who has worked on it, as well as the three wavy lines. It is a practice borrowed from Meissen and Fürstenberg. Unfortunately, it is not always possible to pair the marks with known painters during the first 75 years, since some marks are single letters, others numbers. After 1850 marks were entered alongside names in the company's books. Still, the old marks give some guidance.

In several cases it is possible to identify the different styles and specializations of painters by their marks if not their names.[83] Painter 7 for example specialised in the Onion pattern and other decorations on the star-fluted shapes; painter K appears to favour a very unlifelike rendering of flowers; painter = is clearly more at home with the Blue-Fluted pattern than with the more robust Blue Flowers. One painter, using the mark '2', appears in the 1790s as the artist of some excellent bouquets of flowers, sometimes with slender leaves ending in a double hook; this detail is repeated well into the nineteenth century. From the lists kept since 1794 it is apparent that the decoration of Blue Flowers was assigned to only a few painters, whereas the majority worked on the 'Immortelle' decoration of the Blue-Fluted pattern. Particularly interesting to the collector and connoisseur are dinner services produced between 1795 and 1797. These were painted with flowers and insects on plain surfaces by Lars Hansen and Christian Arnborg. The flowers, which show signs of having been painted quickly to prevent the absorption of colour by the bisqueware if the brush lingered, are combined in bunches but not tied with a riband as was the usual practice. They comprise tulips, roses, fringe-petalled poppies, carnations, bindweed, asters, daisies and smaller flowers.

Through the long period of blue painting at Copenhagen, from 1775 (or 1773 if we take account of a few surviving examples of Mueller's experimental work) to comparatively recent times, we see variations of colour and drawing technique which, if they have something to do with the different skills and mannerisms of the artists employed, are also bound up with the complex chemistry of cobalt as a colouring medium.

The Copenhagen craftsmen, like those of the Ming dynasty in China, painted freehand on a porous body, before glazing. But it is an interesting fact that the Chinese, with centuries of experience to guide them, preferred to fire their blue wares once only, in the glazed state. They simply dried the thrown or moulded article before painting, thus ensuring the maximum porosity and absorption. Unlike the Copenhagen painters, who ran their brushes over the surface quickly to prevent the colour being absorbed, the Chinese relied on the porosity of the pot to prevent running of the blue. Even so, they were unable to prevent the precious Muhammadan blue from running,[84] and found it necessary to mix the imported cobalt with a less pure native ore to achieve their remarkably beautiful and rich colours. Of all the European factories, Copenhagen came closest to the Chinese masters in the splendour of the blues which became synonymous with the name of the Danish capital and its Royal Manufactory; but the imperial wares made up until the end of the seventeenth century, when polychrome enamels came into fashion, transcended both chemistry and technique.

It is worth comparing the problems and methods of the European porcelain factories with those of the English earthenware potters who made a special art of blue printing and conquered much of the world market in the nineteenth century with their decorated creamwares, earthen 'pearl wares', and in the case of one of their greatest exponents, Spode, with Stone China.

The historian of Spode, Leonard Whiter, has written: 'The art of engraving was highly evolved before the introduction of blue printing to pottery. But (refinement) . . . was not possible for underglaze blue printing on absorbent biscuit ware until several technical advances had been made.'

The most important advance was the introduction of 'wet' printing, by which the paper used to transfer the colour image from a copper-plate to the ware was 'soft-soaped'.[85] The quality of the paper used for engraved transfer printing was improved too, for female apprentices to cut into constituent parts so that they could be correctly placed on the biscuit vessel and rubbed on with a flannel. An eye-

[82] The factory also produced the 'Blue Flowers' theme in purple on-glaze versions at this time. For example, sauceboat and stand (C5 and 8-1969) and plate (C125-1916) in the collection of the Victoria and Albert Museum, from the bequests of C. L. David and Lt. Colonel K. Dingwall, respectively.

[83] Bayer took refuge from the irksome discipline of the Flora Danica book illustrations during the 1770s and 80s, in painting the blue-decorated wares. Although signed examples of Blue Flowers by Bayer are rare, the initials J.C.B. appear, for example, on a flower pot in the Gisselfeld Collection in Denmark executed prior to 1779. See Grandjean, *Blaablomstrede Stel*, Copenhagen, 1968.

[84] See Garner, *Oriental Blue and White*, p.16, and W. J. Young, 'Discussion of some Analyses of Chinese Underglaze Blue and Underglaze Red', *Far Eastern Ceramic Bulletin*, Dec. 1949. The Persian glazes contained arsenic, but that substance is not found in fourteenth or seventeenth century Chinese wares. No adequate chemical study has been carried out on Chinese Blue and White.

[85] Whiter, Leonard, *Spode*, Barrie & Jenkins, 1970.

ROYAL COPENHAGEN

[86] William Evans, see Whiter, p.141.

[87] Simeon Shaw, *History of the Staffordshire Potteries*, 1829, p.215.

witness account[86] of the process written in 1846 observed: 'The dry and absorbent porosity of the ware aids the adhesion of the colour in the oil (the liquid medium). . . .' Blue colour printing began at Spode in about 1784.[87]

The process was similar to that used by the polychrome decorators at Copenhagen and other porcelain factories to obtain outlines for their work. The blue decorators, however, relied on freehand method and deft brushwork to achieve their objectives. The standard of workmanship necessarily varied.

It must be remembered that the blue-printed wares of the earthenware potters were high fired at the biscuit stage, whereas those of the European porcelain factories were subjected to the *grand feu* only after decorating and glazing. Even at the relatively low temperatures of the earthenware firing cycle, the bisque was much less porous and therefore easier to paint or print. Even so, the Persian potters applied their Kashan blue on a black (manganese) base, to counter absorption.

The curved shapes with their fleeting suggestion of rococo style were discontinued soon after the turn of the century. Plain shapes took over with ozier borders, and the 'Blue Flower' design with its floral bouquet always in the centre of the plates (and usually of dishes and bowls) fell into disfavour. By 1820 Blue Flowers comprised only 14 per cent of blue-decorated wares, against the 69 per cent of Blue-Fluted. In 1821 a tea service in the 'French fashion' appeared, with plain, slender pot with a long curved spout and pointed, bud-shaped knob on its lid. From 1825 there is a French-style tureen with plain upright handles and a 'bud' on the lid, and a plain foot. The architect G. F. Hetsch designed several new models from 1821 and became artistic supervisor from 1828. In 1835 he designed angular coffee and tea services which were decorated on-glaze as well as under the glaze. In 1841 a new 'Renaissance-style' table service was designed by the painter Andreas Juel. The flowers used in these later services differ from those of the Mueller period. The bouquets are denser and appear to have been painted with thick brush strokes. Naturalism and the light tread of the restrained rococo so typical of Copenhagen in its early period had given way to the heavier gilded and more ostentatious styles of a war-ravaged Europe which looked to the machine to revive its fortunes.

49

49 Tea caddy, probably designed by Hetsch. Painter's mark 2N. Large-scale, somewhat stylised bloom characteristic of Hetsch period, c. 1830. Height 5in (127mm). Kunstindustrimuseum, Copenhagen.

50 Tureen with deep cobalt blue under white glaze, though lacking character of earlier glazes and the drawing has coarsened. c. 1820-25. Length about 10in (254mm). Royal Copenhagen Museum.

BLUE AND WHITE

50

ROYAL COPENHAGEN

51 Oval tureen in the rococo style, c. 1840. Painter's mark 2. Overall length 15in (380mm). Royal Copenhagen Museum.

52 Blue Flowers on the curved shape designed in about 1903 by Arnold Krog from pieces produced in the 1780s. The range is still in production, and remains one of the world's most sustained and popular examples of applied art.

53 A Blue Flower plate of the present day with moulded ozier (basket) rim perpetuates the hand work of two centuries.

52

7
Figures

[88] See Hayden, p. 113 *et seq.*, 'a perfect craftsman'.

[89] Grandjean, *Royal Copenhagen Porcelain*, p. 16.

[90] This work also used detail from Luigi Grossi's marble bust of about 1775 and Johannes Wiedewelt's marble study of 1774, which was lost in the Christiansborg fire.

[91] Hayden, p. 105, also points to 20 figures of Norwegian 'types' based on the sandstone figures of Fredensborg as examples of Luplau's versatile skill, as well as models for the Flora Danica service.

[92] Tvede also made the pedestal for the Queen's bust, and was paid 3 rixdollars for his pains. The statuette of Prince Frederik bears the initials of the modeller Andreas Hald, but it is probable that the original model was made by Tvede.

It is widely believed that the appearance of Anton Carl Luplau at Copenhagen in the earliest days of the Mueller period, replete with the experience and knowledge gained in his years as model-master at Fürstenberg, enabled the Royal Manufactory to produce figures of high professionalism from the beginning.[88] In fact, the skills often attributed to Luplau were ambivalent. His reputation at both Fürstenberg and Copenhagen was that of an informed technician but a variable artistic talent whose figures were 'almost impossible to sell'.[89]

Reputations can be misleading, however, especially when they are based on the contemporary views of competitors and subordinates who are long since departed. Luplau was certainly capable of a deft touch, as is demonstrated by his bust of Queen Juliane Marie executed in 1781 (based partly, as already observed, on Stanley's bust[90] of 1776), and in a few surviving figure groups, of which his delightfully impudent commentary on the Europa-and-Bull theme is an example.[91] There is enough originality evident in his surviving works, especially in the porcelain bust of the old Queen, to suggest the confidence and conviction of an artist who is capable of rising to the challenge of commissions worthy of his talents. Certainly there is no evidence that the Queen ever sat for him. Perhaps there was a streak of arrogance in the model-master who had come from the famous German factory to the new and unproven pasture of Denmark. In a letter Mueller wrote to the board of management on one occasion regarding the cost of a figure and Luplau's contribution to it, he remarked: 'He demands extra payment for any work which he does himself, and as the factory cannot afford this most of the figures and moulds are made by Kalleberg, and in this work Luplau appears to take a very small share'.

Statuary such as the bisque portrait of the Dowager Queen and a statuette of Juliane Marie's son Prince Frederik, attributed to Claus Tvede[92] the sculptor and modeller (at the factory 1775-1783) after a design by Grossi, represented rare excursions into the realms of sculpture at Mueller's factory. The glazed and decorated ceramic figure, hostage to the caprices of public taste and commercial whim, is another matter. The technique of slip-casting from piece moulds, which made the porcelain figure a commercial possibility, was used also by the earthenware and soft-paste potters of the early eighteenth century. The advent of hard-paste porcelain, however, was a necessary condition of compliance with the mood of that century.

Technique and substance were ideally suited to the making of delicate figures of elaborate posture, colourfully painted, re-

54 *Biscuit bust of Queen Juliane Marie on gold-ornamented base. Signed LUPLAU FEC: 1781. Height without base 17¾in (450mm). Saved from the Christiansborg fire in 1794. Rosenborg Palace Collection, Copenhagen.*

FIGURES

55 *Europa, a striking version of the mythological beauty and the transmogrified Zeus by Anton Carl Luplau, c. 1780. This is a modern copy of the original, in current production. Height 10½in (267mm).*

55a *Detail from Europa figure group.*

flecting in appendage and suggested movement the essence of the rococo spirit. The artists who made the porcelain figure into the unique expression of that spirit were seeped in its antithesis, the theatrical sculpture of the baroque. But the challenge of porcelain was not in the first place sculptural; it was decorative. The early figures of the great porcelain houses of Saxony, Prussia and Thuringia were table-pieces for the rich, durable substitutes for the *chefs d'oeuvre* of the palace confectioners, those sweetmeat manifestations of the good life – the chase, the hunt, the pretty girl and the floral extravaganza – which provided after-dinner conversational gambits before being broken up and consumed. By the time that porcelain manufacture arrived at Copenhagen, the ceramic figure had achieved at Meissen, Berlin, Hoechst, Nymphenburg and elsewhere the status of an art form. It had supplanted sculpture as the medium through which the spirit of the age was best expressed.

But by then the new classicism had begun to eclipse the mood of which the porcelain figure was the natural exponent.

The influences of the past fifty years were prevalent enough at Mueller's factory. Luplau had left Fürstenberg for Copenhagen at a time when the German factories were still immersed in the comedies of art and nature, their subjects beckoning from scrolled, asymmetric bases. Such influences were absorbed by the Copenhagen factory, but they were not allowed to dominate.

The first English-language historian of Royal Copenhagen, Arthur Hayden, was generous in his praise of the early figures, though making passing reference to the need for 'critical examination of style'. 'The fertility of the early Copenhagen period', he wrote, 'when masterpieces full of charm and perfect in style, rapidly appeared . . . has puzzled students . . .'

Hayden added that Luplau could not have

56 Lunéville biscuit porcelain figure, Shepherd with Kid, by P. L. Cyfflé from a Sèvres original of 1769, itself based on J.-F.-J. Saly's pièce de reception in marble for the French Academy of 1751. Marks 'TDL' (Terre de Lorraine, used on porcelain and terracottas) and 'jacque' (probably a 'repairer'). Height 8¾in (224mm). Dated 1770-75. British Museum, London.

57 Shepherd with Kid, Copenhagen version of the Saly Faun, c. 1781. Height 10½in (267mm). Royal Copenhagen Museum.

58 A modern copy of another Copenhagen version (reproduced in 1965 from original model, c. 1781). Dimensions as for Lunéville version.

ROYAL COPENHAGEN

[93] Mark 'TDL' (Terre de Lorraine) and 'jacque' incised. See *British Museum Quarterly*, vol. 3, no. 1, 1928, p. 38, signed RLH. See also Hillier, *op. cit.*, p. 144, Copenhagen versions. J.-F.-J. Saly in Copenhagen, *Det Nationalhistoriske Museum pa Frederiksborg*, in correspondence with author May 1983. The Frederiksborg Museum possessed two versions of *Faun* group in biscuit porcelain (one of which was stolen in 1974) but neither were of Copenhagen manufacture. Cyfflé's model was based on a Sèvres original of 1769, which in turn was based on Saly's 1750 salon offering. For Cyfflé and Lunéville, see Honey, *French Porcelain*, p. 46-7. Another Copenhagen version of Saly's *Faun* in the factory museum is dated 1800 and signed 'OA' (Ole Andersen). See Grandjean, *Kongelig dansk Porcelain*, p. 99.

created all the figures of the period, at one moment 'classic and precise', at another 'elegant, restrained creations of gaiety and fanciful forms in due subjection'. Luplau's equivocal reputation suggests that there is truth in the supposition that someone else modelled or supervised the modelling of much of the figure production from about 1780 onwards.

The figures themselves provide ample evidence of diverse minds and talents at work. The classical influence of the time is demonstrated by a series of biscuit figures, not least in the Copenhagen version of that eloquent statement in Greek marble the 'San Ildefonso Faun'. The Mueller factory's version, c. 1781 (fig. 57), was probably inspired by a Lunéville group entitled Shepherd with Kid,[93] a rendering by Paul-Louis Cyfflé c. 1770-75 of the 'Faun', the *pièce de réception* offered by the sculptor J.-F.-J. Saly to the French Academy in 1750. Saly worked in Copenhagen between 1753 and 1774, where he was director of the Royal Academy, and his influence on both

59 *The Patriot*, c. 1780. Biscuit porcelain. Height 7in (171mm). Royal Copenhagen Museum.
60 *Bathing Venus*, biscuit porcelain, c. 1780. Height 11in (279mm). Royal Copenhagen Museum.

FIGURES

Sèvres and Copenhagen ceramic sculpture was marked.

Other figures of the time strike much the same classical mood; 'The Patriot' and 'Bathing Venus', for example. But there are many and diverse veins. A series of six military studies (fig. 61) combine a robust and universal view of the soldier and sailor in the heyday of colonialism with a nice blend of national ardour. On the other hand, a peasant woman carrying a basket of eggs and a hen (a copy of which is in the Victoria and Albert Museum, London), demonstrates an almost unalloyed national style which is echoed by similar peasant studies up to the present day (fig. 62). It has the confident, uninhibited quality which – if it sometimes fell short in modelling – would none the less infuse the urbane works of the next two centuries with an instantly recognisable national character.

61 *Naval Officer and Drummer, from series of early figures in naval and military uniform. c. 1792, grey-white glaze. Height 7¼in (184mm). Royal Copenhagen Museum.*
62 *Peddling Woman with Hen and Eggs, c. 1780. Height 6¼in (160mm). Royal Copenhagen Museum. Similar figure in permanent collection at Victoria and Albert Museum, London.*

ROYAL COPENHAGEN

FIGURES

64

It is generally accepted that the inspiration for this mainstream of Copenhagen figure making came from the repoussé worker Kalleberg.[94] Dancers, musicians, lady at tea-table, market woman, fruit seller, military and naval studies: the subjects are the universal life-blood of the ceramic figure, but costumes and character are national. There is neither pretentiousness nor flamboyance. Simplicity, directness and earnestness are the most obvious features. The subjects of the rococo figure, popularised by the great German and Italian factories, abound, but their treatment is characteristically subdued. Perhaps many of these figures, mostly unmarked except for the factory's familiar wavy lines, were modelled by Kalleberg. A few in the same genre, however, bear the mark AH incised or painted. They are the work of Andreas Hald, sculptor and modeller (1781-1797). The incised mark HM found on a polychrome figure of a man in national costume at the Kunstindustrimuseum in Copenhagen represents the modeller Hans Meehl who joined the factory in 1791. Some of the appendages of these early on-glaze enamelled figures nonetheless bear the signs of Luplau's influence, especially in the Fürstenberg-style cupids which adorn some groups.

In the classical pieces as well as these essentially Danish essays there are many talents at work, most of them anonymous. We know of a few, however, from incised marks. A statuette[95] called 'A Hero', in the classical style, is by Jesper Johansen Holm who was trained by the sculptor Wiedewelt. A sculptor known to have contributed to figures in the classical vein, Jacob Schmidt, worked at the factory from 1779 to 1807. He modelled a study known as 'Flora and Minerva', also in the Stockholm National Museum. There is a fine study in the classical manner of two Sea Horses, again at Stockholm, but the artist is unknown. The same anonymity applies to a rare study of a 'Chinese Woman and China-man with Fruit Basket' at Frederiksborg.

[94]See Hayden, *op.cit.*, p.121, researches of Professor Krohn.

[95]In the National Museum, Stockholm.

63 *Lady and Gentleman Dancing. First mentioned in factory documents 1790. This illustration is from a modern copy. Note lacework on dress. Height 8in (203mm).*

64 *Bacchus on Rock. Modelled by A. C. Luplau from an ivory statuette by Balthasar Permoser, c. 1780. Luplau made a similar figure at Fürstenburg in 1774. Height 11¼in (290mm). Royal Copenhagen Museum.*

ROYAL COPENHAGEN

The figure production of the Mueller factory is perhaps the least documented aspect of its work and achievement. By and large, that achievement may be said to have been the establishment of a national style. There was good modelling and bad. There was little evidence of any equivalent of the intuitive brilliance of Bustelli at Nymphenburg, or the versatile genius of Kaendler at Meissen; none of the careless rapture with which Meyer at Berlin captured his own version of the 'Ildefonso Faun' in the shape of a beautifully attired shepherd and bedraggled kid; nor the enchanting sentiment of Blondeau's children at Vincennes. There was nothing of the eighteenth-century magic of Paris, Saxony, Prussia and Naples, or for that matter of Madrid. Yet the magic, creeping slowly northward, would eventually infuse Copenhagen with warmth and drama. In figure making, Mueller and his modellers and decorators laid the foundation for a true flowering of the art a century hence. For it is in the late nineteenth, and indeed in the present century, that the Royal Copenhagen figure – painted on and under the glaze – touches the peaks of artistry. In its earliest years, it was an honest-to-goodness contribution to an austere and sometimes chilly Scandinavian scene.

65 Elephant and Lady, c. 1783, symbolising theme of 'Patience'. Height 5¾in (150mm). Royal Copenhagen Museum.
66 Shepherd Group, c. 1780. Height 7¼in (186mm). Royal Copenhagen Museum.

FIGURES
66

67 *Miners' Group, from Norwegian silver miners at Konsberg, 1780s. Height 6¼in (160mm). Royal Copenhagen Museum.*

FIGURES
68

68 *Peasant Woman from Viig, Norway, one of a series of 21 Norwegian figures modelled between 1783 and 1811, after life-size sculptures by J. G. Grund. Royal Copenhagen Museum.*

8
Interregnum

[96] See Shaw, *History of the Staffordshire Potteries*, 1829. Bone an ingredient of Bow and other soft-paste bodies.

[97] Spode early on described his products as 'Felspar Porcelain'. As early as 1770 an American factory was advertising for animal bone to add to its china. See Whiter, *Spode*, p.26 et seq.

[98] Mankowitz, Wolf, *Wedgwood*, p.134 et seq.

[99] See Wedgwood, Josiah C., *Staffordshire Pottery etc.* p.189 et seq.

[100] 1830-40, Hayden, *op.cit.*

[101] 1831 and 1833 respectively.

[102] Bisqueware statuary at Copenhagen was stimulated by the resumption of French kaolin imports from about 1820 and the subsequent development of pastes using both French and Bornholm clays. See Appendix B.

THE period bounded by the Napoleonic Wars and the Franco-Prussian conflict was one of artistic and commercial decline throughout Europe. The great works of the Copenhagen factory had been created in the last years of absolute monarchy: years during which the truly 'royal' factories of France, the German states, Spain and Italy, Austria and Scandinavia vied with each other in pursuit of artistic respect and financial reward. The French Revolution of 1789, the subsequent declaration of war on Austria and the promise of the National Convention to help all the states of Europe to overthrow their hereditary rulers came at the zenith of achievement at Mueller's factory. But creativity cannot flourish for long in a destructive environment. The factories of Berlin, Dresden and Vienna had declined by the time that guns boomed in the Copenhagen Sound. In a sense the destruction wrought by British guns in 1807, damaging the factory in Kobmagergade and destroying many of its moulds and much of its warehouse, was incidental. Incessant warfare and the advancing tide of the Industrial Revolution were sufficient to ensure the degeneration of the arts and crafts, and of those institutions founded on works of hand and mind.

The eighteenth century had seen the flowering of baroque and rococo art within frontiers of patronage; and it had witnessed the rediscovery of classical art at the very moment of the break up of the old order. Sonata form and symphonic convention were introduced into a world of acknowledged priorities, presided over by an almost mathematical God. The French Revolution substituted symbolism and metaphor for eternal truth. Never again would men write or compose or paint with the same certainty and assurance. God may have become a poet-deity, but revolutionary slogans are not as productive artistically as a good dinner in the present and the promise of ultimate reward in heaven. Napoleon infused a disintegrating Europe with a fleeting sense of heroism, the ideal vehicle for the classicism already waiting in the wings. But Napoleon did not take long to demonstrate that he was only human after all, and his grand vision lasted just long enough for the great men who straddled the centuries – Goethe and Byron, Beethoven and Schubert – to transmute classical images and military heroics into the Romantic movement. The visual arts did not fare so well. Painting and sculpture and their allied crafts could respond to *Sturm und Drang* and the *Eroica* with Greek mythology, but neo-classicism was essentially derivative. It would burst forth again with revivalist ardour, but it was a dead end in the creative sense. For almost three-quarters of a century the picture was one of defiant mediocrity.

England, physically insulated from the effects of European war, though involved in its political and military resolution, was nonetheless able to turn the technical advances of the late eighteenth century to advantage. At the turn of the century an unknown potter of Staffordshire conceived the idea of adding relatively large quantities of calcined animal bone[96] to china and earthen clays to produce a translucent 'porcelainous' body. Spode,[97] followed by others, was to set out on a path which would lead to the virtual domination of some of the world's most important markets by the new 'Bone China'.

Wedgwood,[98] under the leadership of Josiah II, won *succès d'estime* with the new material, but no pronounced commercial favour. That factory's fortunes continued to derive from its Queensware version of the old Creamwares, and the meticulous exploitation of the neoclassical decorations and relief patterns that Winckelmann and other art historians of the mid-eighteenth century had foreshadowed. Other potters, such as Thomas Minton and the Woods and Meakins and Alcocks, would follow on with their various forms of 'China', their 'granites' and blue-printed wares, inspired by a heady mixture of Methodism, the Capitalist ideal and steam power.[99] Europe, torn asunder by conflict, inhibited in the adoption of new industrial techniques and deprived of its creative urge and confidence, fell into the degeneracy of the so-called 'Empire' style. Copenhagen followed Berlin and Vienna and other renowned continental factories into the age of decadence.

In 1824 the Copenhagen factory came under the management of G. Hetsch. From then until the 1880s its work was distinguished only by sporadic endeavour; by occasional attempts to break away from the surrounding atmosphere of banality and gloom. Thick and ugly gilding, prosaic shapes and almost photographic decoration based on landscape and seascape take the place of the imaginative skills of Mueller's diverse team. On-glaze decoration in subdued and often muddy browns became the order of the day. The underglaze blue decoration which, by the end of the last century, had become known far and wide as 'Copenhagen', degenerated. By the end of the nineteenth century it was virtually a lost art.

There is occasional uplift. A painting, on a pot of atrocious shape,[100] illustrates Kronborg Castle (where Hamlet met the ghost of his father). The drawing is technically good, especially of the masted ship which occupies the Sound in the foreground. A plate dated 1827 and bearing the painted factory mark and initial 'J', shows something of the botanical accuracy which culminated in Flora Danica in a floral study occupying almost the entire centre of the piece. The painting, by Jensen, is surrounded by a gilded rim design divided into three quite separate patterns. A few other pieces, mostly plates by 'L' (L. Lyngbye), survive to indicate spasmodic attempts at decoration based on native architecture – Soroe, the famous Danish school, and Christiansborg Castle, for example.[101]

After 1867, when the management was taken over by A. Falck, there was one development of note, the introduction of a series of unglazed porcelain figures[102] in the classical style, based on the statues of Thorvaldsen, the great Danish sculptor (fig. 69).

At intervals during this decadent period commemorative and special pieces were produced from earlier moulds, usually with a lilac or purple coloured ground, profusely gilded and conveying commissioned designs of buildings and people. But such works did nothing to improve the factory's fortunes. By 1880 it was bankrupt of money and ideas.

69 and 69a *A bisque statue in porcelain after Thorvaldsen's sculpture of Hebe, c. 1871. Victoria and Albert Museum, London.*

9
Revival
The Period of Arnold Krog

70 Arnold Krog, architect and ceramic artist. Art Director of the Royal Manufactory, 1885-1916.

[103] Founded in 1863 by August Schiott, an engineer who employed the Englishman William Edwards as his technical manager, and used prisoners from the local jail as pottery moulders.

[104] C. Nyrop, *Tidsskrift for Kunstindustri*, 1888, p.67.

THE almost defunct Royal Manufactory was taken over in 1884 by the publicly-owned earthenware factory Aluminia.[103] It proved, in more ways than one, a fortunate amalgamation.

The man who had directed the fortunes of Aluminia since 1868 was an engineer, Philip Schou: an industrialist of rare perception whose views on art and industry would have found favour among the Victorian protagonists of the arts and crafts in England. He believed that 'heavy industry, with its virtually tireless machinery, tends to create a working population that is continually placed at a disadvantage, and is therefore probably ill suited to our small society, our rather easy-going national character and our democratic development'.[104]

He was convinced that the ideal lay in a marriage of art and industry; in the efficient production of wares in which the hand of the craftsman and the mind of the artist retained dominant roles. Such industrial art should have a national quality, an identifiable style. The merits of the Mueller period, unconsciously acquired, would find overt philosophical support under the Schou regime.

The new manager was a realist, however. If

he was to restore the reputation of the moribund factory, art and commercial viability must go hand-in-hand. A new establishment was built at Frederiksborg, by the castle grounds, in the outskirts of the capital. Workshops and studios were designed and sited to ensure efficiency in production and good working conditions. The latest machinery was installed. From about 1856 there had been important advances in the development of steam power, many of them stemming from England where the Industrial Revolution had gathered pace in the early weeks of Victoria's reign. Pumps and other mechanical devices took over many of the tasks hitherto performed by hand and hand-implement. The evaporation of clay slip, 'blunging' and 'wedging' the clays, plate 'jigging' and pressing, hollow-ware shaping, all were now made more effective and precise by steam-powered machines. Even the age-old thrower's wheel and turner's lathe were replaced in the 1880s by mechanically-driven devices. Many of the most tedious and time-wasting production processes which had grown up over centuries were eliminated. But the essential skills of the human hand, in modelling, shaping, painting, basket and piercing work, and other decorating tasks, remained – as they were to remain ever after – the foundation-stone of the Royal Manufactory's claim to excellence. Perhaps the most important technical advance was in firing. New kilns were installed enabling as many as 15,000 pieces to be fired in a single cycle. Smaller decorating and 'muffle' kilns enabled many different firings of on-glaze decorated wares to take place at the same time, in carefully controlled conditions of oxidation or reduction.

But it was Schou's sensibility in creative matters – a quality not always given to businessmen – which was decisive in rescuing both the name and the reputation of Royal Copenhagen.

In the autumn of 1884, the modernisation of the factory completed, Philip Schou met two Copenhagen artists to seek their advice on the appointment of a man capable of determining its creative future. The painter Thorvald Niss suggested a young architect, Arnold Krog, who had recently returned from the grand tour to Italy where he had been chiefly impressed not by the classical heritage so much as by the maiolica and other forms of faience (earthenware) pottery he discovered there. Within an hour of that meeting Schou was at the home of Krog. On 1 October the young architect began work at Frederiksborg on a temporary basis. In January 1885 he was appointed artistic manager.

On his own admission, Krog knew nothing of porcelain. The national style dear to his director Schou was foreign to the new artistic manager. In his own words, 'the national style didn't come easily to me, despite the fact that I should have had it at my fingertips after working for five years on the decorations for Frederiksborg Palace. I didn't do much better with the early Renaissance, but it was from this that my first pieces were evolved: a little coffee service, which by no means could be termed a success.' It is not known whether the service still exists, but a watercolour drawing is preserved in the factory archives. It was decorated partly underglaze and partly on the glaze in blue and yellow, with snake handles inspired by Italian faience. But it was the blue-and-white, on which the manufactory's fame chiefly rested, that first challenged Krog's sensitive skills to a systematic attempt to restore former glory at Copenhagen. He turned first to the 'Immortelle pattern'. We have already seen (p. 64) his testimony to the effect which that pattern had on him when he first glimpsed it, 'the dreamy indigo blue that lay within, melted together with the body'. Outside influences were just as powerful, however, in turning his attention to blue-decorated wares.

Chinoiserie formed an important plank in the platform of the pre-Raphaelites and the voluble arts movements of the late nineteenth century in England. Collecting the blue Ming was a badge of good taste in the Aesthetic Movement. Drawing in the style of the Chinese ceramic artists was a formative influence on serious painters and cartoonists, from Burne-Jones and Whistler to Beerbohm and Beardsley. Had not philistine athletes at Oxford thrown Oscar Wilde's precious 'blue' from a Magdalen window into the Cherwell river, to the everlasting chagrin of the writer?[105]

As it happens, Krog and Schou together visited London[106] at the end of June 1885 at what might be called the meeting point in time of pre-Raphaelism and *art nouveau*, 'that strange decorative disease',[107] and the impression made on the Danes was stressed by Krog in a biographical account. The fact is hardly surprising. England in the 1880s reverberated to the noise of debate as to the meaning and direction of Art. Ruskin, Morris, Whistler, George Moore, Pater and Oscar

[105] Hillier, *op.cit.*. It is difficult to resist the punnish *bon mot* which Hillier says Wilde 'inexplicably' failed to deliver: 'If I had served my God as I served my Ming, he would not thus have left me naked to mine enemies'.

[106] Helsted, *op.cit.*, p. 38.

[107] Amaya, Mario, *Art Nouveau*, 1966.

Sources: Helsted, Dyveke, 'Arnold Krog and the Porcelain' in *Royal Copenhagen Porcelain*; and Hayden, *op.cit.*, Chapter VIII.

Arnold Krog b. 1856, son of a master founder at Frederiksvaerk iron foundry. Graduated Academy of Fine Arts Copenhagen 1880. While a student worked as pupil to leading architect Ferdinand Meldahl, a 'despotic taskmaster', for whom he worked on interior restoration of Frederiksborg Palace, following fire of 1859. See Helsted, *op.cit.*

ROYAL COPENHAGEN

71 Water-colour drawing by Krog, 1885, for coffee-cup, in a revived version of the 'Immortelle' pattern with lace border. Factory archive.

REVIVAL: THE PERIOD OF ARNOLD KROG

Wilde, to name but a few of the eager participants, were nothing if not articulate. But it was not the breezy embrace of *art nouveau* nor the solemn tread of the Gothic revival that moulded Krog's view of the way forward at Copenhagen. It was, rather, an exhibition of Sèvres porcelain which he saw on his way home, at Antwerp. His retrospective account of that experience portrays both his balanced artistic judgement and his grasp of technicalities of which he was totally ignorant a year earlier. Two vases in particular attracted his attention. They 'formed the germ of the new trend I began to follow as soon as I got home'. The vases were tall, slender and decorated with entwined nasturtiums and, wrote Krog, 'The leaves were blue, quite pale, with delicate gold edgings. The flowers were a brilliant coral red'. Two identical Sèvres vases in the display in Antwerp were, he said, all that he could remember of foreign modern porcelain 'that made an indelible impression on me'.

There was a note of humility in Krog's account of the influence of these French pieces on his thinking. 'Now, 40 years later, I can see them quite clearly in my mind's eye. When I returned from my travels I immediately started to experiment in this direction: the blue (the ordinary blue of our immortelle pattern china) was admirable and much more beautiful than that of Sèvres, but the red of their flowers was quite beyond our reach.'

Side by side with Krog's revival of the famous Immortelle pattern, there began designs in the Sèvres manner, with deep, gem-like enamel colours. The French factory used glaze colours (fritted colouring oxides mixed with the glaze), and in the 1880s began the development of its *porcelaine nouvelle*, a heavily felspathic paste which could be fired at a lower temperature than the kaolin-enriched hard-paste to give a marvellous unity of intense enamel colours, glaze and body. The new porcelain was about to sweep the ceramic world. For the moment, however, innovation lay with the Copenhagen factory and its art director, aided by the technical consultant Adolphe Clément, a brilliant chemist. Together they achieved something which had eluded even the Chinese in a thousand years of incomparable achievement in the decoration of porcelain. They developed a glaze with high alkalinity which permitted chrome green and gold red to be fired under the glaze at the intense temperature of the *grand feu*, between 1,400 and 1,500 degrees C. Thus it became possible, for the first time in the history of porcelain manufacture, to fire colours derived from chromium and gold under the glaze, along with cobalt blues and the derivatives of copper oxide. Soon vases and other decorative items exhibiting the delicate gradations of underglaze blue, which were hitherto the speciality of the finest French porcelain, also became part of the Royal Copenhagen range. At the same time Krog and Clément perfected the techniques of underglaze and on-glaze decoration used together to provide subtlety of colouring and remarkable, three-dimensional visual effects (fig. 72).

72 *Vase with mouse, blue and gold underglaze decoration with on-glaze gold, decorated by Krog in 1887. Height 3in (75mm). Kunstindustrimuseum, Copenhagen.*

By late summer 1885 Krog was searching far and wide for new ideas and inspiration, turning often to particular pieces of delft and maiolica, and then perhaps looking back over the Mueller period and the indifferent interval to find designs worthy of revival or of modification. Inevitably the 'Blue-Fluted', or 'Immortelle' pattern as he preferred to call it, occupied his mind. By late 1895 he had made several improvements to versions of the famous design which had become distorted and anaemic over the years. Others were changed completely. 'I got to grips with it, and tried to create forms that were suitable for covering with the decoration that had been established for years. I was adamant in my demands. . . .', he wrote. By 1887 he had produced a galaxy of experimental forms decorated with the 'Immortelle' pattern.

Such forms included a paraffin lamp; a small dish in which a new boldness of decoration is circumscribed by complicated circular and triangular shapes and elaborate perforation, and an 'insect' handle (fig. 41); and a coffee cup and saucer each standing on small feet formed as part of the scale pattern (fig. 71).

Within a few months of his appointment, Krog was in the throes of the revival of the service, which was still labelled Mussel in the factory, and was officially called Blue-Fluted. From the foundation of a single plate from the old service, as we have seen in Chapter 6, he created an entirely new luxury service with richly perforated lace borders. With the help of Clément and the painter Oluf Jensen he was to make it the most famous and sought after luxury service in the history of western porcelain. By 1887, within two years of his joining the company, green and red on-glaze versions were being produced in addition to the standard underglaze decoration. Within a decade the largest section of the decorating department was engaged in the painting and piercing of thousands of pieces every year for the leading shops of the world. Krog brought the decoration back to its early precision. It was faithful to Mueller's original pattern, but not a slavish copy. Krog and his artist assistants responded to the spirit of their century, as had their predecessors (see figs 38-44).

Soon after joining the factory Krog was invited to visit Paris by the wealthy collector and connoisseur William Salmonsen.[108] It was another milestone in the art director's appraisal of the contemporary direction of the applied arts and of their applicability to the national style he was determined to restore to Copenhagen. He was able to see 'the extraordinarily bold way in which the Japanese and to a certain extent the Chinese decorate their things. There are no rules, no styles, everything can be used: a volcano and a spider, a falling leaf and a Persian arabesque, everything is possible because it is used with complete artistic understanding of what is decorative. It is like a solo against a soft accompaniment – there is always a single patch of colour, a single motif that produces the effect. As little as possible, but as full of character as possible – and never conflicting with the rhythm of the form itself. For me it was a complete revelation.'

Krog had found another guide to action, *Japonisme*, chiefly through a sight of the collection of the Franco-German art dealer Samuel Bing who had spent a year collecting 'the most perfect things' from China and Japan before it was too late 'to reap the rich harvest' which his knowledge and business acumen combined to predict. In 1895 Bing opened a shop called L'Art Nouveau in the Rue de Provence, at the centre of the new art craze. Krog returned to Copenhagen to give practical expression to the pervasive mood of Paris in the last decade or so of the nineteenth century.

Several drawings made by Krog in 1886 for the guidance of the art and production departments show plants, grasses and butterflies after Japanese motifs. A number of jars of the period are decorated in the Japanese manner. A small lidded jug, of which a sketch survives, was painted with birds against gold fans which Krog himself thought 'very good'. Salmonsen purchased it immediately. In 1887 Krog used an illustration of two fish in a Japanese manual for young art students as the theme for a dish featuring a bird, a ship's sail and fish hanging from the branch of a blossoming tree (figs. 73 and 74). In September 1888 a Japanese-inspired decorative piece of the period, a vase depicting a sea wave on the point of breaking, was completed. It was based on one of the coloured woodcuts, 'The Wave', in *A Hundred Views of Fuji*, produced by the Osaka master Hokusai.

Whatever the impact of the Japanese style on Krog, however, its absorption into the Copenhagen scheme of things was invested with the subdued tones of underglaze decoration, and with the unpretentious quality which was the essence of a factory approach based on the creation of a distinctive character in its *Kunstindustri*.

At a Scandinavian Exhibition of Industry, Agriculture and Art held in 1888 at the Industrial Association in Copenhagen, the fruits of the first three years of Krog's artistic direction were on show. The Great Exhibition in Paris the following year, at which the factory was awarded a Grand Prix, enabled the world at large to see the results of Krog's early efforts.

[108] According to Krog's own memoirs 1886, but diary of Philip Schou in factory archives suggests 1888. See Helsted, *op. cit.*, note 6.

REVIVAL: THE PERIOD OF ARNOLD KROG

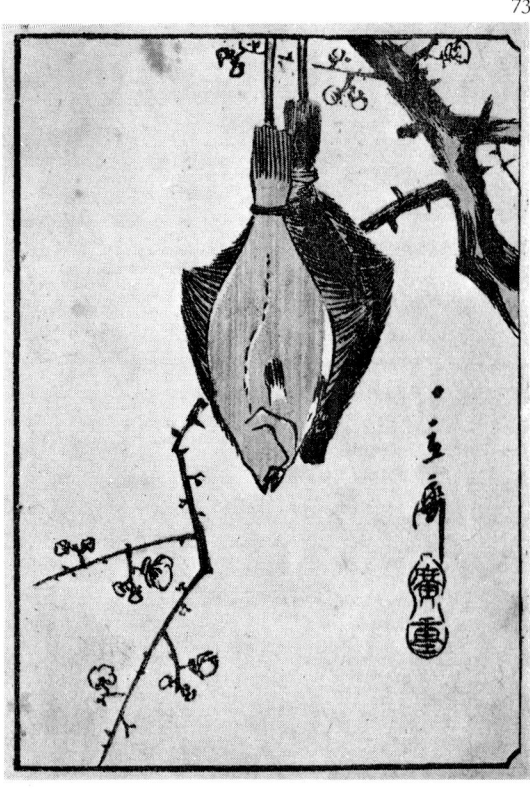

The director of the Sèvres Museum, Edouard Garnier, wrote in the *Gazette des Beaux-Arts*:

> Nothing, however, could be simpler than these pieces, which aroused great admiration from the very first day: a touch of blue, sometimes a suspicion of red, a little gold – that's all. But the blue is so mild, so fastidious – indeed elegant – and the green and red so gently harmonious, the material so beautiful, and these few ingredients applied with such great decorative understanding and deftness, at times even boldness, that they have sufficed to enable M. Krog to create these unique works.[109]

[109] *Gazette des Beaux Arts*, II, 1889.

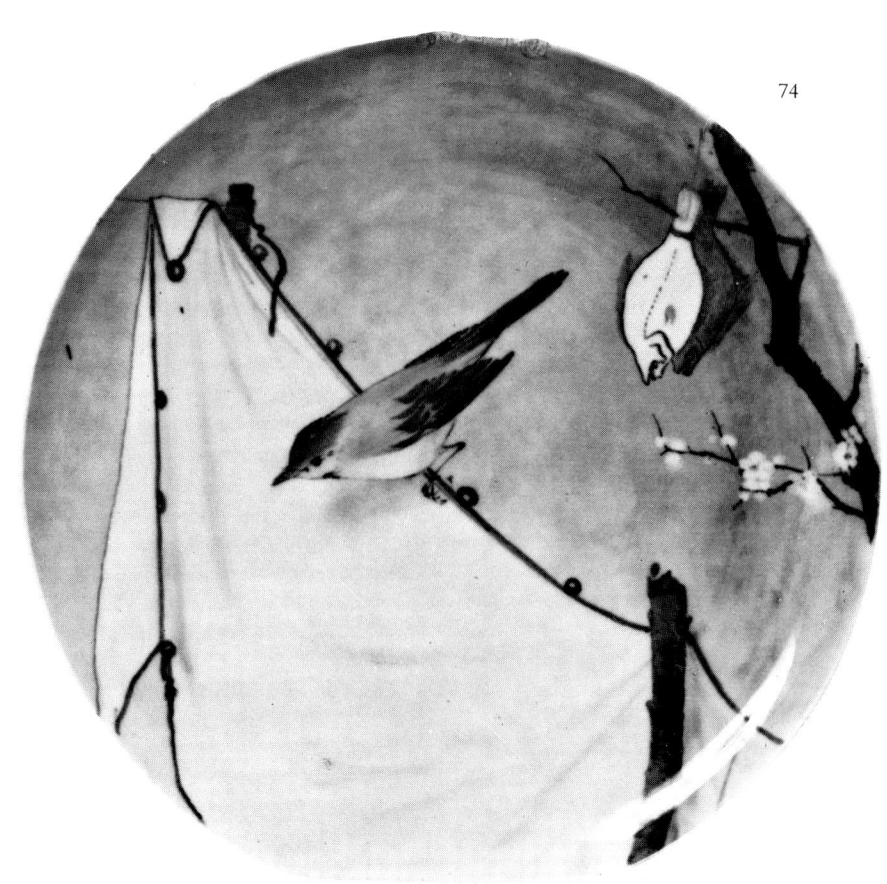

Comparing Krog with the French master of applied art Emile Gallé, the critic Roget Marx wrote: 'In Copenhagen as well as in Nancy, it is the surrounding countryside which acts as a source of inspiration and guide; in other words both M. Krog and M. Gallé uphold the

73 *Illustration from Japanese guide for drawing students, inscribed with publisher's name and 'Hiroshige', c. 1850. Used by Krog for experimental dish in fig. 74. Factory archive.*

74 *Dish decorated by Krog in 1887. Blue-painted underglaze. Kunstindustrimuseum, Copenhagen.*

ROYAL COPENHAGEN

[110] *Revue des Arts Décoratifs*, 1890-91.

[111] Notable artists in the decoration of these pieces were V. Th. Fischer, G. Rode, C. F. Liisberg, F. A. Hallin, Chr. Thomsen, Stephen Ilssing and Benjamin Olsen.

[112] Krohn, Pietro, *Tilskueren*, 1900, pp.687-88.

fine principles of the Japanese in accordance with their own mentalities and their own climates'.[110]

There was an explosion in the 1890s of the naturalistic, underglaze blue-decorated vases and plaques which were to become another distinctive feature of the range. By the mid 1890s the Royal Manufactory had produced a range of porcelain table services and decorative pieces which surpassed the output of any other European factory, in extent and in a rare combination of decorative restraint and versatility.[111]

In 1896 came the scallop-edged service, and in the period 1894-99 the Marguerite service was produced in time for the World Exhibition at Paris in 1900. A contemporary writer in the Danish periodical *Tilskueren* wrote:

> . . . a couple of flowers appear in barely visible relief on the faintly scalloped edge. A single bumble-bee, a dragonfly or a grasshopper forms a handle or grip as required. The colouring is just as simple. The porcelain has a slightly reddish, soft, creamy tone against which the few flowers stand out white – that's all. . . . It is quite simply the most beautiful service in the exhibition, *sans pareil*. . . .[112]

75 *Dish decorated by Krog in blue, red and green underglaze with on-glaze gold, 1886. Royal Copenhagen Museum.*

REVIVAL: THE PERIOD OF ARNOLD KROG

In this *furore* of creative activity, Krog found time to breath new life into the most famous of the old factory's patterns. In 1906 he began to recreate the original models of Flora Danica, which had departed considerably from the intentions of Mueller and the execution of Bayer and his colleagues in the late eighteenth century. The work based on the pearl design had been produced spasmodically at the Kobmager Street factory to the end of its days, with chrome colours as used on the Queen Alexandra version instead of the copper hues of the original. The use of the more varied palette was continued, and remains the rule to the present day. The old principle of choosing plants for scientific fidelity has given way over the years to aesthetic considerations, though the illustrations of particular plants remain true to the book. The old practice of specifying on every piece the number of the engraving from which it was drawn and the part number of the botanical work, has been abandoned: only the Latin name of the plant is now painted on the reverse, in black. An exception is found on some of the pieces painted by Krog after 1906. They bear the so-called

76 Coffee pot and cup and saucer in Marguerite service, designed by Krog in 1897, decorated in pink and grey under the glaze, 'insect' handle and knob.

[113] Several new models of the 'pearl' design on which the Flora Danica was painted, were made at the old factory from 1862, and at Frederiksborg from 1885 under Krog's direction. A list of the items is given in Grandjean, *The Flora Danica Service*, note 46.

[114] Madsen, Karl, *Tidsskrift for Kunstindustri*, 1887.

Queen Juliane Marie mark – the blue wavy lines surmounted by a crown.[113]

'Blue Flower' decoration was also given a new impetus under Krog's regime. There had been an earlier revival in 1868, the year in which the factory employed its first woman painter. Curved shapes were reintroduced, and from that date two distinct types of decoration were adopted, the original centrally placed motif on the Ozier (basketwork) services, and a new Meissen-influenced 'side-bouquet' on the curved shapes. The flowers in the latter related to the Saxony on-glaze blooms, though not as naturalistic, and were tied with a clover-leaf riband. In 1903 Krog introduced new models for the Ozier service (Blue Flowers, plain shape, as the catalogue has it). In 1913 he designed a new angular shape for Blue Flower, based on a Hetsch coffee service of 1835.

Various experiments carried out by the chemist Engelhardt, intended to emulate the old clays of the Mueller period with their grey tinge so much admired by Krog, were unsuccessful. The Bornholm clay, replaced by the clays of France (and later England) to achieve Krog's icy white paste, was used once again for some of the blue-painted wares, especially by Oluf Jensen. He achieved results almost indistinguishable from the Mueller wares in his rendering of the 'Immortelle' and 'Blue Flower' decorations.

From 1906, also, dates the introduction of porcelain figures and table services based on the best of the old factory's work. In the former category, the work of the new factory surpassed that of Mueller and Luplau in both variety and modelling. An ardent Danish folk tradition permeated the style: meticulous, highly professional modelling based on the imaginative observation of nature was to lay the foundation of one of the finest figure ranges of the modern world. Again, underglaze decoration was to provide an intrinsic discipline. Danish life, from peasant figures deriving from the factory's eighteenth-century studies to perennial favourites such as the 'Goose Girl', 'Boy with Calf' and 'Swineherd', many of them modelled by the prolific Chr. Thomsen, would become part of an international language of figure design. Animals by such modellers as Erik and Frederik M. Nielsen and Theodor Madsen combined artistic acceptability with commercial popularity. The plumage of a bird, the dress of a human, the colours of the animal world may in reality have a thousand hues. Copenhagen, uniquely, subjected the polychromatic world of life and nature to the constraints of underglaze decoration, often of a single colour – blue or a dash of red or brown. It is a discipline which has been widely copied in the twentieth century, but seldom equalled in its sculptural quality, or in the subdued charm of its decoration. Inevitably, the fairy-tale stories of Hans Andersen provided subject matter for the modellers. 'Princess and Swineherd', 'Soldier and Witch' and other literary inventions were realised in original and finely observed and detailed studies of book illustrations, in *blanc de chine* and underglaze colours, to stand alongside the figures of another tradition – elaborate, often exotic on-glaze enamelling, as in Henning's 'The Princess on the Pea' study. Some of the finest figures of the period were modelled by Krog himself.

In 1909 Krog designed a Fan service with blue underglaze border based on a motif which he had long kept in mind. He opened up an eighteenth-century fan. 'The relief work on the surface was to all events excellent, a pretty variation on the flute motif of the immortelle pattern plate. I went up to the modeller's workshop with my drawing and old Jacobsen said he thought it could be made.' That was soon after Krog joined the factory. If anything materialised at the time it has not survived. But the Fan service of 1909 remains in production to the present.

'Kunstindustri', said the Danish art historian Karl Madsen, 'is actually an odd word – it has the body of a woman and the tail of a fish.[114] Arnold Krog gave it meaning in an age when the word 'industry' was despised by artists, and when 'art' was seldom more than a description of a necessary evil to industrialists.

On 18 March 1931 Professor Arnold Krog celebrated his 75th birthday amid tributes from the directors of the great museums of the world, and fellow artists of craft and industrial potteries. Among the words of approbation published by the *Tidsskrift for Kunstindustri* to mark the occasion, the following from Bernard Rackham, director of the Ceramics Department of the Victoria and Albert Museum, put the man's remarkable achievements in a nutshell:

> The importance of Mr Krog's achievement rests not only, perhaps not chiefly, in what has been produced by himself and his staff of fellow artists. It consists also in the impetus he gave to new endeavour in other quarters. Far beyond the boundaries of Denmark the effect is apparent. In many other countries also

REVIVAL: THE PERIOD OF ARNOLD KROG

technical experiment has gone hand in hand with artistic invention in the output of new vital works of art in porcelain; and in other techniques also, in faience and stoneware, there has been a revival. . . . of public interest in the ceramic arts for which recent years have been remarkable. Never before perhaps in Europe has pottery been so seriously regarded as a material for artists to work in, nor have the public been slow to give encouragement to their essays. . . . For this healthy revival thanks are due in a very large measure to the Danish artist to whom at the age of seventy-five we are glad to give our tribute of congratulation.

He retired as art director of the factory in 1916, but continued to work as adviser and creative inspiration until 1931. Even after a near half-century in the thick of ceramic art, however, he acknowledged that the most formative influence on his work had been the Paris Exhibition at the turn of the century.

77 Coffee pot, sugar bowl and cup and saucer in Fan service, designed by Krog in 1909. Blue decorated under thick creamy glaze.

10
Crystal Glazes, Stoneware and Art Faience

SHORTLY after the Scandinavian Exhibition of Japanese arts and crafts of 1888, the Danish historian Karl Madsen wrote:

> China's porcelain manufacturers occupy a place of honour amongst all their colleagues as the greatest colourists.... Imitation of this is no doubt an extraordinary sign of the times. The beauties which characterise it are precisely the beauties which make the strongest impression on modern, over-refined nerves.[115]

It was a reminder of a simple truth which was being lost sight of in the helter-skelter pursuit of the Japanese art pottery which had begun with the opening up of the Japanese ports to the West in 1854. The Scandinavians were fortunate in being able to show at their exhibition pieces loaned by Samuel Bing, for his (and Bernard Hirschprung's) collection of Japanese pottery was the only worthwhile assembly of that country's ceramics in the western world at the time. Europe and America had been set alight in the last two decades of the nineteenth century by revelations of the wonders of Japanese applied and decorative art. The great museums of the two continents began to build up collections which were based largely on the evidence of that 'rapacious and indiscriminate'[116] collector Edward Sylvester Morse, of whom the twentieth-century historian Soame Jenyns was to write: 'In effect he accumulated a vast conglomeration of second- and third-rate material, much of it the work of amateurs or from almost unknown provincial kilns, while the pieces he fondly believed to be from the hands of the great Japanese potters like Toshiro or Ninsei, may possess their stamp or signature, or Ninagawa's[117] attribution, but can be dismissed almost without exception as palpable imitations.'[118]

It was on the strength of Morse's collection and evidence – his catalogue was published in 1901 – that the European craze for Japanese ceramic art was principally founded. But Krog on his visit to Paris in 1886 (see note 108, perhaps 1888) had doubtless been shown Bing's much more expert and discriminating collection, and the factory's chief chemist Clément had probably seen the famous Oriental collection of the Parisian connoisseur when he visited France in 1885.[119]

Be that as it may, it was the explosion of interest in Japanese pottery and the passion for Oriental art in general, which inspired first Sèvres and then other European factories to set off in pursuit of the *art du feu*, and which manifested their influence at Paris in 1900 in the form of the Sèvres *porcelaine nouvelle* and stoneware. The effect on Krog and the art directors of other factories was electrifying.

There is confusion in the minds (or at any rate the writings) of experts in regard to the technical background and the definitions of clay bodies and decorative mediums through which Europe set out to emulate the jewel-like colours of the great Sung dynasty wares of China, and the derivative works of the Japanese. It is a confusion which centres on definitions of 'porcelain' and 'stoneware', and which calls into question the entire western habit of giving imprecise names to ceramic materials.

It was artists such as Gauguin and Van Gogh who provided the stimulus for French leadership in the European search for *l'art du feu*. It was Van Gogh who in a letter to his sister declared that he would build up his picture 'de la couleur brillante, bien arrangée, resplendissante'.[120] Gauguin was preoccupied with the very process of firing pots in the *grand feu* so that in a single application of the kiln's flames to a colourless clay object it emerged blazing with colours of indescribable beauty. 'Et voyez comme la nature est artiste.' He found in this transformation of nature's own raw materials 'toute une méthode d'harmonie'. It was stoneware that gave Gauguin the

[115] *Tidsskrift for Kunstindustri*, 1888, p.11.

[116] Jenyns, Soame, *Japanese Pottery*, Faber and Faber, 1971, p.2 et seq.

[117] Ninagawa Noritani, celebrated nineteenth-century antiquarian.

[118] W. B. Honey of the Victoria and Albert Museum wrote of 'This huge ridiculous Morse', Jenyns, *ibid*. Morse's collection was sold to Boston Museum in 1890 for 26,000 dollars.

[119] Helsted, *Royal Copenhagen Porcelain*, note 9.

[120] *Verzamelde Brieven van Vincent van Gogh*, IV, Amsterdam-Antwerp, 1955, p.160.

General source, Merete Bodelsen, *Royal Copenhagen Porcelain, 1775-1975*, p.59 et seq.

78 *The Potter by Jais Nielsen, made life-size in stoneware for the Paris World Exhibition of 1925.*

CRYSTAL GLAZES, STONEWARE AND ART FAIENCE

ROYAL COPENHAGEN

[121] Bodelsen, Merete, *Gauguin's Ceramics*, Faber & Faber, 1964, p.190-91. But Hillier, *op. cit.*, 'Gauguin wanted to use the clay for making everything but pots.'

[122] Salmonsen, *Kunstbladet*, 1888.

[123] Bodelsen, *op. cit.*

[124] Hayden, *op. cit.*, p.295, 'Copenhagen produced the first Crystalline Glaze'. See Bodelsen, *Copenhagen Porcelain*, p.65 et seq.

The historian of the Royal Doulton factory, Desmond Eyles, attributes the pioneering of the crystalline glazes to 'the Royal Copenhagen ceramist Clément'. See *Royal Doulton 1815-1965*, Hutchinson, 1965, p.158.

[125] See Bodelsen, *op. cit.*, p.59 et seq.

[126] Bodelsen, *op. cit.*, p.59.

[127] To put it another way, 'felspathic stonewares of a more or less porcellanous nature', J. G. Ayers, sometime keeper in the Ceramics Department, V & A Museum, on Sung Wares.

clue to the true subtlety of colour, 'built up abstractly and yet in obedience to the laws of nature.'[121]

But it was porcelain coloured by *flambé* glazes with which the artist was to become most familiar through sharing in the studio of his friend and mentor Ernest Chaplet, whose work created great interest among connoisseurs when it was exhibited in Paris in the autumn of 1887. The Danish collector William Salmonsen visited the Chaplet display but every piece had been sold before he arrived. He was able to purchase a few pieces, however, from the French potter's workshop, which he took home to Copenhagen and showed to a small circle of ceramic craftsmen, who found them 'most attractive indeed'.[122]

Chaplet had taken Salmonsen on a conducted tour of his kilns and laboratory 'where he keeps his many different enamel colours with their corresponding samples and where he works and experiments every day with a view to achieving the ideals he seeks in the play of colours presented by precious stones'. Arnold Krog, it will be recalled, had visited Paris with Salmonsen, and Clément had made an earlier excursion to the scene of intensive experimentation in the new glaze colours. Another distinguished collector of Oriental wares of the time, also known to Krog, was Bernard Hirschsprung. Emil Hannover wrote of him: 'In Denmark he admired Arnold Krog, in France Chaplet, Massier, Delaherche, Dalpayrat, Lachenal and the great master of glass, Gallé.... Surely there never existed a more tender relationship between a piece of stoneware and a human being....'.[123]

It seems that the stoneware, which sought to recreate the marvels of the Sung potters in an interaction of clay, glaze, colour and fire, and the new porcelain with its crystalline glaze colours (such as the Sung and Ming potters had developed empirically), fired at a relatively low porcelain temperature, were spoken of in the same breath in the most exalted collecting circles. One thing was certain, if Sèvres was the first to carry out serious experiments with either technique, Copenhagen was privy to many of the carefully preserved secrets of the French factory. Indeed, the English writer Hayden was to claim that Copenhagen invented the new glazes, a fiction which was to be perpetuated into the latter half of the twentieth century.[124]

Crystalline glazes

The immense success of Krog's revived underglaze decorated wares at the Paris Exhibition of 1900 was rivalled by the appearance of the Sèvres *porcelaine nouvelle*.[125]

The French factory produced crystal glazes on some of the largest vases it had ever made in one piece, thus – in the words of one contemporary writer – demonstrating 'who was the master and who the apprentice'.[126] In the simplest terms, Sèvres, after years of experimentation, had achieved a porcelain paste which, by dint of a lower glost firing (1,350 degrees), could carry enamel glazes with strong, deeply translucent colours.

The body was of the felspathic type characteristic of much of the Chinese paste which, although technically translucent, was often opaque to the eye when fired and could, in western terms, be regarded as a stoneware or stone china with as much justification as porcelain.[127] The secret of its glowing, jewel-like glazes lay in the addition of zinc oxide and quartz to the glaze colours.

Clément began to experiment with the synthesis of crystals in the porcelain kiln at the factory in 1886, shortly after his return from Paris. Some of his earliest crystals were donated to the Mineralogical Museum of Copenhagen where they can still be seen.

When the minerals used by Clément were added to the ceramic glazes, however, they failed to crystallise because of interaction with the clay body. In 1888 the technical manager of Royal Copenhagen was presented with a ready-made chemical and ceramic guide. Lauth and Dutailly of the Sèvres factory published in the *Bulletin Chimique* an account of the *porcelaine nouvelle* with complete details of the formulation of the new glazes. Clément made copious notes from the article which showed how, by using silicates of zinc, they had produced 'small prismatic crystals'. Different colouring effects were achieved by the addition of various metallic oxides. Clément noted that larger crystals were formed by slow cooling in the kiln. The original contribution of Copenhagen to the new techniques lay in Clément's discovery that the process could be applied to the existing hard-paste body. It did not require the reconstituted felspathic paste of the French factory, which permitted a lower glost firing temperature.

Clément fired the colour-glaze on top of the pre-fired porcelain in the oxidising atmosphere of the muffle kiln. The basic glaze was alkaline and particularly refractory. For the

CRYSTAL GLAZES, STONEWARE AND ART FAIENCE

79 *Porcelain vase with* oeil de chat *glaze by Valdemar Engelhardt, 1897. Designed by Arnold Krog. Factory mark and C602 VE. Exhibited in Paris 1900. Height 6¾in (172mm). Kunstindustrimuseum, Copenhagen (previously in collection of Bernard Hirschsprung).*

second firing in the muffle kiln (which took place at the same high temperature as the first) the frit of quartz and zinc oxide, together with the colouring oxides, was brushed on. According to Clément's notes remarkable results were achieved. Nickel, for example, which normally produces only brown tones, gave a beautiful Persian blue when introduced into the zinc compound. Unfortunately, none of Clément's original crystalline pieces survive. According to him, the first vases with the new glazes went into production in 1889, and according to one observer they were shown at the Paris *Exposition* of that year. Factory records do not confirm that claim, however. The first mention of crystal glaze wares is in connection with a consignment sent to the factory's depot at Bing's premises in Paris in March 1890. On that date 120 vases 'with coloured glazes' were despatched.[128]

The following year Clément left his employment at Copenhagen following a dispute with the management. It was left to his successor, the chemist Valdemar Engelhardt, to take up his work. From that moment, Engelhardt's kiln logs provide a complete record of the progress of the crystal-glazed wares. By 1892 pieces numbered 1 to 267 (it seems that the Clément pieces bore serial numbers starting at 251 and ending at 370) were drawn from the kiln. Forty-two of the Engelhardt pieces went to Paris and 23 to Chicago. Alongside the entry for no. 164, the name G. *Vogt, Sèvres*, appears.

Production increased year by year as did the variety of glazes. In 1894 a selection of vases was sent to the Sèvres Museum, and its director Edouard Garnier congratulated Engelhardt on his 'beautiful glazes'. A year earlier the factory had presented its new glazes 'showing the most peculiar *grand feu* colours' at the Chicago World Fair. In the same year Mr Brooks of Chicago visited the factory and was 'simply delighted' with the crystalline glazes. In August 1894 Mr Louis Tiffany and his brother-in-law Mr Forrest turned up at Copenhagen. They were 'delighted with our glazed ware, some of which they regarded as being absolutely superb', according to Philip Schou.

Factory records describe the brilliant and varied range of colours achieved by Engelhardt in the 1890s. Flamed blue, pale yellow flamed, onyx, celadon-green, blue marbled, yellow, yellowish-brown, pink and bluish-green, are all referred to, but never as 'crystal glazes'. Engelhardt himself used the terms 'Coloured glazes' and 'Flamed glazes'.[129] There is a confusion of numbering in the Engelhardt period, in which alphabetical prefixes and decimal points are used, but the earliest numbers which refer specifically to 'crystal' appear to be 366 'blue-crystal' and 369 'cobalt-crystal'. The factory's Paris shop used the term *flambées* to describe these multi-coloured wares. Chaplet, when he visited the shop in Rue Rossini in May 1890, objected to the designation and suggested the term *coulées* or flow glazes.

In the Victoria and Albert Museum there are numerous late nineteenth-century vases[130] with the factory mark and the initials VE (Valdemar Engelhardt), which clearly show the range of colours and decorative effects achieved by the use of zinc oxide and quartz (silica) to produce silicated glazes. There is also a group of French studio and Sèvres pieces with which they can be compared.

From Engelhardt's log it is possible to follow the gradual mastery of colour and glaze effect. Such entries as 'bright yellow, dark crystals' and 'grey opal, a few blue spots' in 1892, are followed by a note of the first *l'oeil de*

80 *Porcelain vase, similar in shape to fig. 79, with green crystalline glaze by Valdemar Engelhardt, c. 1890. Factory mark and DANMARK under crown in green, VE in monogram and E101 in blue and A134D incised. Victoria and Albert Museum, London.*

[128] Bodelsen, *op.cit.*, p.66 and note 23.

[129] English potters, especially at the Doulton factory in Staffordshire where experiments with copper-red and crystalline glazes began in the 1890s, referred to the former as 'transmutation' glazes, a term used in connection with the *flambé* and *sang de boeuf* of the Sung, Ming and early Ch'ing periods. Copper oxide glazes were fired in reducing atmosphere in the muffle kiln. It was not until the early years of the present century that the Royal Doulton factory began to produce crystalline glazed wares on a 'special high-temperature ceramic body', described as an 'extremely difficult technique of which the Royal Copenhagen ceramist Clément had been the pioneer' (see note 124). 'The crystalline glazes were an artistic triumph but not an economic proposition'. Eyles, *op.cit.*, p.158-9.

[130] Reserve Collection.

CRYSTAL GLAZES, STONEWARE AND ART FAIENCE

81

82

81 *Sèvres* porcelaine nouvelle *vase with turquoise glaze, 1880. Victoria and Albert Museum, London.*

82 *Porcelain vase by Ernest Chaplet, with crimson glaze; a four-sided composition with white edges. c. 1900. Victoria and Albert Museum, London.*

ROYAL COPENHAGEN

83 Copenhagen crystal-glazed porcelain vase, 1897, streaked with pale green. Factory mark and C765 in blue, D plus cross incised, VE in monogram. Height 6¾in (172mm). Victoria and Albert Museum, London.

84 Crystal-glazed porcelain vase, c. 1900. Factory mark and F874/K2 impressed. Victoria and Albert Museum, London.

CRYSTAL GLAZES, STONEWARE AND ART FAIENCE

85 *Vases with crystalline glazes, 1900-10, designed by Arnold Krog and glazed by Valdemar Engelhardt. Left, shape 1887, glazed with blue 'snakeskin' 1910, height 7½in (190mm). Centre, shape 1890, matt white crystalline glaze 1900, height 9½in (240mm). Right, shape 1890, glazed reddish-brown and black, 1900, height 6in (152mm). Royal Copenhagen Museum.*

chat glaze in 1893. The *craquelé* technique was gradually mastered, in snakeskin grey, Persian blue and reddish-brown. The new effects were well suited to the mood of the last decade of the nineteenth century, and an *art nouveau* range emerged of diminutive frogs posing on water-lily leaves, dragonflies, crabs and other subjects from nature. A frog on a leaf encircled by a grass snake was sent to the Sèvres Museum, and Garnier its director responded enthusiastically to the 'exemple soit suivi par des modernes ceramistes'. Later larger animals, especially polar bears, were modelled as part of a developing versatility in the new medium, wandering round the edges of large, crystal glazed ash trays, or pondering an ice-covered lake.

Paris 1900, where the Berlin factory also exhibited the crystalline-glazes, marked the high point of the new fashion. After it, many other factories began to experiment in the same field. It was a fashion ideally suited to *art nouveau* ceramics with its glowing and often exaggerated colours. In 1903 M. Taxile Doat of Sèvres wrote in an article on 'Grand feu Ceramics': '... the Danish chemists very loyally acknowledged that it was Sèvres that had drawn their attention to the crystal glazes'.[131]

[131] Adalbert Klein in *Keramos*, 1966, says that research into the crystalline glazes began at Sèvres as far back as the middle of the nineteenth century. See Bodelsen, *op.cit.* p.72.

ROYAL COPENHAGEN

[132] Jenyns, *Japanese Pottery*, p.9 et seq.

Stoneware

Another outcome of the Paris Exhibition of 1900, and of the overwhelming influence of the Sèvres display on that occasion, was a reawakening of Europe's interest in stoneware. It was a revival which owed much to the Japanese wares that had come to Europe in the latter half of the nineteenth century with the force of revelation. The so-called *temmoku* teawares with their iron-brown glazes splashed and mottled with treacly amber and other shades – inspired by the Chien wares of China – had a particular appeal for European eyes.[132]

But there were other influences which doubtless spurred the Sèvres revival. At the Paris Exhibition of 1867, the English factory of Sir Henry Doulton had shown some thirty vases in salt-glazed stoneware, much of the design work done by students of the Lambeth art school associated with the Doulton

86 *Stoneware jar by Patrick Nordström. Semi-matt copper glaze, deep blue, red and purple ('plum bloom'). c. 1914-16. Factory mark and PN in monogram and S754. Bronze lid, chased by Georg Thylstrup. Height 7in (178mm). Kunstindustrimuseum, Copenhagen.*

CRYSTAL GLAZES, STONEWARE AND ART FAIENCE

concern. Their efforts were 'generously commented upon' by French art critics.[133]

Nevertheless, by the turn of the nineteenth century Sèvres had achieved spectacular feats with a ceramic body which had been largely the province of craft and studio potters until the French factory began its experiments in what remained 'secret' and carefully guarded methods of firing and glazing.[134]

Paris in 1900 was alive with stoneware. Even the facades of the Grand Palais were covered with immense reliefs in the long-neglected material. A vast animal frieze in stoneware stood before the main entrance in the Place de la Concorde. Inside, the works of the great French studio potters, such as Chaplet, Delaherche, Dalpayrat, Dammouse, Cazin, Jeanneney and Hoentschel, glowed with what, for most visitors, were colour glazes of almost unimaginable subtlety. Here

[133] Eyles, *op.cit.*, p.66.

[134] Chaplet, who gave up painting in favour of pottery, was probably the first European ceramic artist to produce *flambé* glazes after the manner of the Chinese, prior to 1860. For some years he worked with Emile Lessore, who adapted old engravings to underglaze decoration before moving on to Minton and (1858-75) Wedgwood where he worked in the Renaissance style. The most profound Orient-inspired influence on European potters, however, was exerted by Théodore Deck from his workshop in Blvd. Montparnasse. Deck became briefly director of the Sèvres factory in 1887, but died in 1890. See Deck, Th., *La Faience*, Paris, 1887; Burton, Wm, *Porcelain*, London, 1906.

87 Stoneware jar with blue-grey rutile glaze over slip, by Nordström. Signed PN in monogram and 1-4 1919 I. Private collection.

105

ROYAL COPENHAGEN

88 *Stoneware jar by Axel Salto with 'Sung' glaze. Height 16in (400mm).*

89 *Stoneware bottle by Nordström, 1918. Almost black glaze flowing into* sang-de-boeuf. *Height 7in (172mm), unique piece. Royal Copenhagen Museum.*

CRYSTAL GLAZES, STONEWARE AND ART FAIENCE

was the true *art du feu*. Of the European factories only Sèvres, heir to a surviving craft tradition and surrounded by suitable high-firing clays, had mastered it. Stoneware was the potter's material, challenging and rewarding in its ability to transmute colouring oxides according to the wiles of nature rather than the preconceptions of man. Nobody was more entranced than Royal Copenhagen's art director Arnold Krog. He returned to Denmark determined that the factory would master the art of stoneware manufacture.

Progress was slow. Tentative efforts were made with a body based on the refractory clay used at the factory for lining the ball mills, a blue clay which could be used effectively for faience (earthenware) manufacture but which proved unsatisfactory for stoneware.[135]

Valdemar Engelhardt took charge of the technical side of the experiments, and the artist-modeller Knud Kyhn the artistic. The modelling of animal sculptures, at which Kyhn himself excelled, was often outstanding. The practical achievement was unremarkable, however, which is perhaps surprising. Soon after the Paris Exhibition Georges Vogt of Sèvres had published a detailed account of body formulation and glazes. The glaze colours were obtained in the same way as those used in the *porcelaine nouvelle*, bright colours being achieved by firing in an oxidising atmosphere, subdued and matt effects by reduction firing, often with 'rutile' added to the glaze. Vogt[136] suggested that other factories might henceforth improve on the Sèvres methods. Krog's team at Copenhagen does not seem to have taken his benevolent prompting to heart; in the beginning at any rate it was happy to copy French techniques and styles.

It was not until a more suitable clay was discovered in about 1906 on the island of Bornholm that real progress was made, but even then the expertise had to be sought else-

[135] Bodelsen, *Royal Copenhagen Porcelain*, p.73 et seq.

[136] Vogt, Georges, *Notice de la fabrication des grès*, l'Union Ceramique et Chaufourniere de France, Mourlot, Paris, 1900.

The term 'stoneware' is another of the ill-defined inventions of the West. 'Blue' or 'ball' clays found in many parts of the world are, in fact, the basic ingredient of stonewares, though the addition of china stone (felspar), or felspathic clays, is often necessary. There are many variations of the body but its essential feature is a high degree of vitrification at temperatures of 1,250–1,300 deg. C, and an ability to form a chemical unity with colouring oxides and glaze in the *grand feu*.

90 *Animal group, Lioness with Young*, by Knud Kyhn. 'Sung' glaze, c. 1920.

91 *Stoneware Hippopotamus by Knud Kyhn, 'Sung' glaze. First made 1928, still in production.*

CRYSTAL GLAZES, STONEWARE AND ART FAIENCE

92 Pontius Pilate. Figure group in stoneware by Jais Nielsen, with sang-de-boeuf *glaze. First made 1927, last copies produced 1982.*

where. The studio potter Hans Hjorth was given the task of working with the Bornholm clay, and it was he who produced the first Royal Copenhagen stonewares.[137] Philip Schou had left the factory by then, and his place as managing director was taken by Frederick Dalgas, a man who like his predecessor had a ready appreciation of both technical and aesthetic problems and was able to give inspired leadership to the factory's artists and craftsmen. He tried to persuade Hjorth to join the factory but that potter preferred to remain independent.

Not until 1912 was it possible for Copenhagen to establish a stoneware department worthy of the name within its own walls. It was then that a self-taught craftsman potter named Patrick Nordström came on the scene. Nordström brought his own vitrifiable stoneware clay, his own glaze materials and his own methods. He guarded his book of glaze recipes, which he always kept in his pocket, and weighed out all ingredients personally. Within a few months of his joining the factory examples of the Copenhagen stoneware were on show at the Danish Society of Arts and Crafts Exhibition of 1912.

The explanation of Nordström's remarkable ability to rival the best stonewares of Sèvres and of the great French studio potters was for many years a mystery to his employers. His work at his own premises at Bakkegardsalle in Copenhagen (1902–7) was known to them. But his reputation was that of a maker of indifferent earthenware pieces with garish, alkaline glazes.[138] At Vanløse (1907–10) he had used ready-made German clays and glazes in the production porcelain wares. He had worked at Paris at the time of the 1900 Exhibition.[139] Arnold Krog wrote that he 'knew all the old masters of the 1880s personally: Chaplet, Delaherche, etc. all the

[137] Some of these early pieces exhibited at the Artists' Autumn Exhibition in Copenhagen, 1908, as 'Figures in Stoneware. Glazes by V. Engelhardt'.

[138] Bodelsen, *op.cit.*, p.77.

[139] As a stucco worker.

109

93 Stoneware vase by Axel Salto, with 'Olivin' glaze, 1943. Height 8in (203mm).

[140] Obituary notice 1929.

[141] L. Auclair, pp.97-108. Among papers left by Nordström were tracings of pots by Carriès and Chaplet, reproduced in the same issue of *Art et Décoration*.

[142] Republished in German, *Sprechsaal* Vol.34, 1901. Taxile Doat in *Art et Décoration*, Sept. and Nov. 1906, and Feb. 1907.

[143] Nordström continued working in retirement until the year of his death in 1929.

modern ceramic pioneers . . .'.[140]

In fact, his sources of information were close at hand. An article about the great French ceramic artist Carriès appeared in the journal *Art et Décoration*[141] in October 1910, in which the Frenchman's collaborator Auclair revealed details of body clays, glazes and firing techniques. A footnote in that article led Nordström to an account in the same journal during 1906-7 of Sèvres methods by Taxile Doat, which elaborated on the revelations of Vogt in 1900.[142]

Thus, Nordström had ready to hand a complete account of chemistry and techniques. From 1912 until his retirement[143] in 1922 he produced a marvellous array of stoneware bowls, jars and vases, and animal figures modelled by Kyhn. He used both slip and brushed-on glazes, experimenting endlessly with the materials which his mentor Carriès and the Sèvres factory had used to such effect. And he extended their achievements into realms which he made his own, and which gave to the Copenhagen factory another and most significant claim to fame in the Arnold Krog period. An astonishing variety of colouring and glazing materials were employed: basalts, lavas, copper and iron, rutile and uranium, copper and uranium, iron and rutile, wood ash; each formulation given a number on its shelf so that mathematical combinations could be contrived and the results noted. The uniquely tactile, luminous quality of stone clays in unity with colours created by intense heat and flame acting on the carefully formulated glazes, gave rise to some of the finest examples of applied art of the twentieth century – items which could stand alongside the finest works of the Mueller period or the best of Krog's porcelain.

Plum bloom, *sang de boeuf*, *flambées*, violet aubergine, *poumon de cheval*: the colours and effects created by Nordström the Swede in the tradition of the stonewares of Sung and Ming and the Japanese artist potters provided a rich new vein for the Royal Manufactory to mine.

During his managership of the stoneware department, Nordström acquired the services of an outstanding potter, Carl Halier, who succeeded him in 1922. And in his last two years at the factory he took on another assistant, Jais Nielsen, who was to become one of the finest and best known of Danish stoneware potters. Knud Kyhn, his earliest collaborator and one of the best of all pottery animal modellers, was to continue at the factory until his death in 1969. Among others who came after Nordström and who made important contributions to the renown of Copenhagen in a field which was rich in artistic, if not financial, reward were: Axel Salto, Kresten Bloch, Gerd Bøgelund, Jørgen Mogensen, Helge Jensen, Nils Thorsson, Mogens Andersen and Ivan Weiss.

CRYSTAL GLAZES, STONEWARE AND ART FAIENCE

94 Stoneware vases by Nils Thorsson with sang-de-boeuf *glazes. c. 1970.*

Art Faience

A twentieth-century development born of the merger of the Aluminia factory with the Royal porcelain manufactory in 1884, was a range of art wares in the earthenware or faience body which quickly became a byword of design in a variety of styles appropriate to the changing moods of the age.

Many extraordinary claims have been made for these wares which range in their decorative treatment from luscious floral studies to simple geometrical designs; and in shape from elaborate and heavy Hispano-Moresque type vases to the simplest rectangular ash trays. The polychromatic tin-glaze wares generally labelled *maiolica* and *delft*, and the earthenwares of Faenza in Italy (from which the name 'Faience' derives), have been suggested as decorative prototypes.

In fact, the Copenhagen Art Faience wares were the outcome of progressive management giving an opportunity to artists of diverse talents to work with a minimum of restriction on a body[143] which can be fired at a relatively low temperature and decorated freely on or within its slip glazes.

The results have been a tribute to the factory and its artists since the range was inaugurated in the 1920s under the management of Frederick Dalgas.[144] The first head of the Art Faience group was Christian Joachim who combined a sense of national style with a catholic approach to matters of design in general which from the outset gave these decorative pieces a particular appeal to Danes and yet ensured a world-wide following. Early subjects under Joachim's direction were old favourites of the porcelain factories, Harlequin and Columbine; Clown; Bottom, Puck, Oberon and Titania, Philostrate, Flute and other characters from *A Midsummer Night's Dream* (of which figures Joachim himself, R. Harboe, and H. Slott Mueller were the chief modellers and decorators); *bonbonnières*, vases, ash trays, simple bowls and jars. These wares have been marked from their inception with the letter 'A', representing the Aluminia side of the partnership formed in the nineteenth century, crossed by the three lines of Royal Copenhagen.

The work of the Art Faience department has from the outset owed a great deal to Nils Thorsson whose long life-span embraced some of its best early designs and its most recent achievements, a few of which are illustrated in the following pages.

[143] There is no specific 'earthenware' body composition. Earthenwares vary from coarse milled flints to the relatively fine but impure 'blue' clays which are the basic ingredients of Copenhagen faience. They are fired to a temperature approaching that of the vitreous stonewares.

[144] Son-in-law of predecessor Philip Schou.

95 *Early Art Faience by Christian Joachim, dish polychrome decorated under the glaze, 1903. Diameter 18in (450mm).*

CRYSTAL GLAZES, STONEWARE AND ART FAIENCE

95

11
The Modern Factory

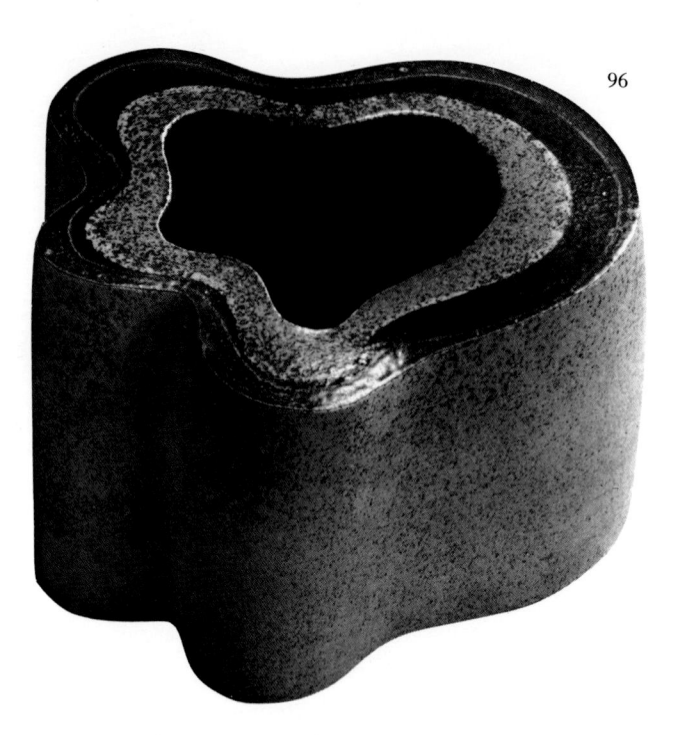

96 Stoneware vase by Bente Hansen, 1980.

THE chapter heading is, in a way, misleading. The Royal Copenhagen Manufactory is neither ancient nor modern. It is, as it always has been with the exception of inevitable but brief periods of depression and decadence, a factory of the present.

It neither looks to the past reverentially because it is the past, nor to the future out of misplaced zeal for 'modernism'. For more than two hundred years it has abided by the essential rule of excellence: that its appeal to the collector, the connoisseur and the ordinary user of its products should be based on a cosmopolitan view of the world at large informed and enlivened by an honest national style. Emotive and pejorative phrases such as others use to stress longevity or adherence to current philosophies in art and design – terms such as 'traditional' and 'contemporary' – are seldom if ever used at Copenhagen. If the factory's wares are assessed in the context of the art and industry of the past quarter of a millennium it will surely be judged that its fine tableware designs and disciplined decoration of the twentieth century are no less admirable than the works of hand painters in the eighteenth century.

When William Burton came to make his wide-ranging contribution on 'Ceramics' to the famous Eleventh Edition of *Encyclopaedia Britannica* in 1911, he reserved praise for Royal Copenhagen which was in marked contrast to his general stricture:

> Artistic results. – While the great potteries of Europe have been employed in improving their methods of manufacture and in consolidating their knowledge of the technical and scientific side, so that they are able to produce pottery more perfect in shape, with a higher degree of finish and greater certainty of result than was ever known before, it cannot be said that the artistic results have been commensurate with the labour expended.

But of Copenhagen, whose ascendancy he believed arose from the Japanese influence

THE MODERN FACTORY

which followed the Paris Exhibition of 1867, he wrote:

> The most admirable result of this revived interest in Japanese art, however, developed at the Royal Copenhagen works, the productions of which are not only famous all over the world, but have set a new style of porcelain decoration which is being followed at most of the continental factories. By the use of the pure Swedish felspar and quartz and the finest china clays from Germany or Cornwall a material of excellent quality is prepared, and on this naturalistic paintings of birds, fishes, animals and water or northern landscapes and figure subjects are painted in delicate under-glaze blues, greys and greens. The Royal Copenhagen works has also produced a profusion of skilfully modelled animals, birds and fishes, either in pure white, or delicately tinted after nature, with the same under-glaze colours. Not only have Berlin, Sèvres and other European factories adopted the modern Copenhagen style of decoration, but Japanese are now imitating these skilful productions which were originally inspired by their own early work.

Burton may have exaggerated the influence of the Japanese Collection shown at Paris.

97 *The Princess on the Pea, a fairy-tale inspiration for a study in elaborate figure modelling and immaculate enamel decoration, by Gerhard Henning. First made in 1911. Still in production. Height 17in (425mm).*

ROYAL COPENHAGEN

[145] See Hillier, *op.cit.*, ref. to J. K. Huysmans' *L'Art Moderne*, ed. Lucien Descartes, VI, in which Kate Greenaway, Walter Crane and Randolph Caldecott are seen as the pioneers of the new simplicity, all illustrators of children's books.

Krog, the virtual founder of the factory's twentieth-century reputation, was greatly impressed by the very selective Oriental collection of Samuel Bing in Paris; but the effect of his visit to Paris in the 1880s was to create in the factory's potters and ceramists an awareness of the Chinese gems from which Japanese porcelain and stoneware arts and the arts of the 'flow' and 'transmutation' glazes derived. The testimony of the distinguished contributor to *Encyclopaedia Britannica* represents a fair account of the position and influence of Royal Copenhagen, however, as it gathered up the threads of eighteenth-century creativity, and made for itself a foundation in the century of world war and bewildering technological change: the century in which the clamorous 'art movements' of the past gave way to bellicose and assertive 'design' philosophies.[145]

Copenhagen was no more the captive of the Bauhaus and its didactic architectural and typographic disciplines than of the art move-

98 National Costume Figures, from island of Amagar, by Carl Martin-Hansen. Height 13½in (343mm). First made 1906, still in production.
99 Moongirl by Gerhard Henning. Porcelain decorated on the glaze. First made 1924, still in production. Height 12in (300mm).

99

ROYAL COPENHAGEN

ments through which it had passed since its inception in the eighteenth century, or the more banal excesses of the present era. In his *Pottery and Porcelain 1700-1914*, Bevis Hillier wrote apropos the *art nouveau* period:

[146]Hillier, *op.cit.*, p.335.

> In Copenhagen, Thorvald Bindesbøll, son of Gottlieb Bindesbøll, the architect of the Thorvaldsens Museum . . . made ceramics which anticipate modern design more, perhaps, than those of any other *art nouveau* potter. Herman Kähler's lustre decoration at Nestved, Denmark, and the painting of Carl Mortensen and Gerhard Heilmann on Copenhagen porcelain, all belong to the more austere *art nouveau*. Copenhagen was the least reactionary of the great European factories. Its icy paste, so suitable for models of polar bears, penguins and sea gulls, is still in use, and modern Copenhagen models are virtually indistinguishable from those illustrated in Borrmann's *Moderne Keramik* of 1902. Here, too, the Japanese influence was strong: Borrmann illustrates a 'Vase, Moven und Meerswelle, nach einem motif des Hokusai gemalt von Arnold Krog (1888)'.[146]

There were 'peacock' plates of course, just as in the 1930s there were excursions into the mannerisms of *art décoratif*. But there was no dominant *art nouveau* period, just as there was no rococo or neo-classical dominance in earlier centuries; or jazziness or crankiness amid the extravagances of cubist experiment and Odeonesque architecture. Such movements and experiments were absorbed, but with the exception of the decadent styles of the mid-

100

'Krog bought a few modest Japanese things from Bing (c. 1886) including a couple of woodcuts made by an Osaka master about 1830.' They were signed Shunkosai Hokuei (sic). See Helsted, *op.cit.*, p. 50 and n.11.

100 *Icelandic Girl by Arno Malinowsky*, blanc de chine, c. 1931. Height 6¼in (160mm). Victoria and Albert Museum, London.
101 *Weeping Faun by Gerhard Henning*. Porcelain decorated on the glaze. First made 1910, still in production. Height 6¼in (160mm).

101

ROYAL COPENHAGEN

THE MODERN FACTORY

102

nineteenth century, they were always subordinate to a national decorative ethos. There was no essentially geometrical style in the twentieth century any more than an essentially floral or landscape period in the eighteenth to nineteenth centuries such as characterised some of the English factories in the great days of Derby, Worcester and Coalport; nor a devotion to invented Oriental themes as in the *chinoiserie* of the early 'Indies' patterns of Staffordshire and the 'delftware' factories. Good design, fine modelling, a keen observation of nature, and artistic freedom within the confines of those disciplines necessarily imposed by the different pottery bodies which came into everyday use – earthware, stoneware and porcelain – became the twentieth-century guidelines.

The decal and lithographic transfer which came into almost universal use in the second half of the present century never imposed their sameness of decoration at Copenhagen, except as a means of providing guidelines for painters in some of the more complex patterns, only exceptionally to supplant the artist's hand when sameness of pattern was desired.[147]

If evidence were needed of the Royal Copenhagen contribution to applied art and design in the present age, it is surely to be found in the perpetuation of the great patterns of the past – 'Flora Danica', 'Immortelle' and 'Blue Flowers' – and in the 'classical' modern tablewares at the other end of a broad spectrum. It is found too in a figure range which conveys in one breath the exotic charms of the Arabian Nights and Hans Andersen's fables and fairy tales in underglaze colours and immaculate on-glaze enamels, and in an animal world in which the nuances of posture and movement are captured with a sculptor's eye, and colour and texture by the imaginative use of underglaze colours – never by an attempt to achieve the impossible, the representation of fur or feather with the enameller's brush. And to stress the versatility of modelling and decoration alike, there are the national costume figures of Carl Martin-Hansen, and the daringly improbable alliance of classicism, orientalism and mythology in the figures of Arno Malinowsky and Gerhard Henning in the 1920s and 1930s.

[147] A few current patterns in the tableware range are decorated by lithographic methods.

102 *Figures by Malinowsky. On-glaze decorated porcelain. Mermaid, 1926, 10in (254mm); Flora, 1926, 11¾in (300mm); Dancing Bali Girl, 1924, 11½in (286mm).*

121

ROYAL COPENHAGEN

103 and 103a *Chessmen: Crusaders and Saracens.* Porcelain, on-glaze decorated, by Siegfried Wagner, 1913. Still in production. Height 4¾in to 8in (120-203mm).

104 *The Rock and the Wave by Professor Theodor Lundberg, 1899. Still in production.*

The stoneware art established under Nordström's secretive aegis has become a perpetual challenge to new generations of craftsmen, who still use three of his specially formulated glazes: the mottled so-called 'Gundestrup', the greyish-white and iron-brown 'Sung' and the red *sang de boeuf*. Nils Thorsson, one of the earliest craftsmen of the stoneware department, celebrated his 60th jubilee in 1972. He created innumerable shapes for the new glaze formulations, with the fish (applied by ingenious brushwork and slip-ground techniques) as a favourite theme. His inventiveness also contributed to Joachim's Art Faience range which, under his (Thorsson's) guidance, developed during the 1950s into the unique decorative range of gift and commemorative items known as 'Tenera' and 'Baca'. Stoneware and porcelain with the crystalline glazes were produced into the 1930s and beyond by Christian Joachim, Nils Thorsson, Jais Nielsen, Knud Kyhn, Carl Halier and a host of other gifted potters and ceramists who had learnt their various crafts under Nordström and in the creative hothouse of Krog's regime. Artists of the highest calibre, such as Jeanne Grut, Axel Salto, Ellen Malmer, Mogens Andersen, Ivan Weiss, Eva Staehr-Nielsen, Anne-Marie Trolle, Bente Hansen, Gerd Bøgelund and Gerd Hiort Petersen, have added to one of the finest traditions of western ceramics, and extended it into the realms of modern sculpture (figs. 105-114 following, text continued on p. 131).

105 *Elephant and Deer in stoneware by Knud Kyhn, modelled in 1957 and 1942 respectively. 'Sung' glaze. Height each 8in (203mm). Still in production.*
106 *Stoneware vase by Mogens Andersen, made in 1973. Height 38in (965mm).*

106

ROYAL COPENHAGEN

107 *Stoneware vessels by Snorre Stephensen, 1979. Still in production.*

108 *Stoneware series by Ivan Weiss, 1974. Still in production.*

ROYAL COPENHAGEN

109 *Stoneware bowl by Axel Salto. 'Sung' glaze. First made in 1949. Height 3½in (90mm), width 4¼in (108mm).*

THE MODERN FACTORY

110 *Flask and vase by Nils Thorsson. Flask (height 7in, 178mm) first made in 1958. Vase (height 3½in, 90mm) first made in 1956. Both vessels decorated with Solfatara (uranium) glaze.*

ROYAL COPENHAGEN

111, 112 and 113 *Stoneware pieces by Bente Hansen, 1981-82.*

114 *Diana. Pieces from the extensive range designed by Nils Thorsson in the last years of his life, 1970-75, for a 'porcelainous' stoneware body decorated with plant and animal subjects.*

THE MODERN FACTORY

Of Nils Thorsson's later works a stoneware range known as 'Diana' demands attention (fig. 114). Subdued brown and rutile glaze colours on a body with a high felspar content, which gives it the character of some of the finest Oriental stone bodies, are highlighted by blues, reds, yellows and greys in decorations which embrace delicately painted naturalistic themes. 'Diana', introduced in 1977, has given popularity to a potter's art which was hitherto the almost exclusive province of the expert and the collector. Another highlight of the art faience and stoneware studios within the factory is Jeanne Grut's famous 'Blue Fish', wonderfully modelled in an earthware body with incised and blue slip-glaze decoration. Based on the long-lost and rediscovered *coelacanth*, it is one of the most distinguished examples of twentieth-century naturalistic figure modelling (fig. 156).

114

ROYAL COPENHAGEN

A table service modelled by Christian Joachim in 1912, the pattern 'Tranquebar' (fig. 115) with a bold blue flower motif within painted basketry, has been extended in recent years by the addition of green, red, and brown versions; in the latter the original tulip bloom has been replaced by a flower of the primrose family.

Grethe Meyer's best-known excursion into tableware, her 'Blue Line' faïence range of 1962, is evidence, if such were needed, that the earthenware body at Copenhagen is not a substitute, a poor man's porcelain. High fired in the bisque kiln, with a delicate blue-grey glaze and immaculate hand-painted edging it is a classic of present-day design, eternally of the present. It has the glassy resonance of porcelain such is the degree of its vitrification. And it has the shapes of well-proportioned, disciplined sculpture (fig. 116).

115 *Christian Joachim's Tranquebar service in the* faïence *body was translated to red and green versions in 1976, retaining the bold tulip-flower of the original and the fine border basketry. There is also a brown version with a primrose floral motif.*

116 *Blue Line, by Grethe Meyer, 1962. Architectural precision in shape, immaculate potting in an earthenware body, and a rich blue-grey glaze, with a single hand-drawn blue line on rim.*

THE MODERN FACTORY

116

An essay exhibiting the same restraint in design, though this time in the porcelain body, is Anne-Marie Trolle's much-praised Domino service (fig. 117), introduced in 1970. Simple lines and dots make up its disciplined decorative theme. Both Blue Line and Domino are seminal examples of twentieth-century design at its best and, predictably, have been emulated by many 'modern' designers in other fields ranging from pottery to plastics.

There have been many other examples in both faience and porcelain of a purity of approach to shape and decoration, from Gertrude Vasegaard's creamy 'killed' glaze 'Capella' made for the factory's 200th anniversary celebrations in 1975, to Snorre Stephensen's blue-glaze teapot with brass handle made a year earlier, and Arje Griegst's conch-shell fantasy, 'Triton' (fig. 118). Such works are exemplary of the present; yet they exist within the context of a factory and a design team which has its roots in the same soil as nurtured Mueller and Bayer and Krog, and generations of Danish craftsmen. The blue underglaze commemorative plates of today began as 'Christmas' plates in 1908 in the era of Arnold Krog, and though painting styles may change there is an identifiable continuity. Bisque medallions and figures; underglaze blue smoking pipes (in which the Immortelle and Blue Flower themes of old are imaginatively adapted to their various shapes); floral themes from the past given a new lease through relief moulding and changing floral motifs (such as the cream-glazed porcelain Frijsenborg tableware); commemorative bowls to mark the great occasions of the present, which bridge the years back to the Battle of Copenhagen: the inventiveness of the second half of the twentieth century is as prolific as at any time in the past.

The search for talent and new ideas is unceasing. In 1969 the Danish court jewellers, A. Michelsen, were absorbed by the factory and there followed a range of jewels which have become outstanding examples of design of the present in their combination of porcelain and precious metals. In 1975 the great Danish silversmithery of Georg Jensen, whose fertile skills had contributed to some of the earliest stoneware, was integrated with Royal Copenhagen.

Art and industry have been served well by many of the great porcelain houses of Europe from the first decade of the eighteenth century. Some have achieved higher things and more widespread fame for brief periods. But none can claim so formidable a history of continuous excellence. The progressive idealism of the Copenhagen factory is as apparent in the present as at any time in the past. That, weighed over more than two centuries, is a salutary recommendation.

117 *Domino. Porcelain service by Anne-Marie Trolle, with disciplined decoration using simple dots and bands in brown, issued in 1970. A design on the same shape, 'Indigo', was issued in 1975 as part of the Royal Copenhagen bicentenary commemoration.*

118 *Triton, a fantasy for the modern table based on the conch shell, designed by Arje Griegst in porcelain with 'rose' colour decoration under the glaze. Relief moulding, 1978.*

THE MODERN FACTORY

118

ROYAL COPENHAGEN

Commemorative and Annual Wares
and other Presentation Pieces

119 *Porcelain plate made to mark coronation of King Edward VII in 1902. Victoria and Albert Museum, London.*

120 *The Gate to King's Garden (Rosenborg Palace), in the 'Portraits of Old Copenhagen' series inaugurated in 1978. This is a revival of an indifferently illustrated series issued between 1830 and 1840 known as 'Copenhagen Prospects'. Porcelain.*

121-124 Historical Plates. *Inaugurated in 1975 to mark the bicentenary of Royal Copenhagen. Porcelain.*

121 *Bicentenary plate. (1975)*
122 *The Declaration of Congress, July 4, 1776. (1976)*
123 *Hans Christian Orsted, pioneer of electromagnetism. (1977)*
124 *Captain Cook, marking discovery of the Sandwich Islands (Hawaii) in 1778. (1978)*

THE MODERN FACTORY

121
1775 1975

122
1976
In CONGRESS, July 4, 1776
The unanimous Declaration of the thirteen united States of America

123
1777 · 1977
HANS CHRISTIAN ØRSTED

124
1978
HAWAII
1778
JAMES COOK

137

ROYAL COPENHAGEN

125-127 Year Mugs
125 *First of the year mugs, produced in 1967 from design by Nils Thorsson; a tradition kept up since by the Scandinavian art faience team, and occasionally by other artists.*

126 The 1979 mug by Ivan Weiss.

127 The 1981 mug by Ellen Malmer.

THE MODERN FACTORY

128

128 The Artist's Egg, an annual limited edition in porcelain since 1975; by Robert Jacobsen.

129-132 Mothers' Day Plates. *Begun in 1971. Artists: 1971-77 Arne Ungermann, 1978-82 Ib Spang Olsen. Underglaze blue-decorated on moulded relief pattern. Porcelain.*

129

130

131

132

139

ROYAL COPENHAGEN

133-150 Christmas Plates. *Probably the most sought-after of all modern commemorative pieces, the Royal Copenhagen Christmas plate is produced in unspecified quantity, and the moulds broken immediately after production. Underglaze blue decoration on relief-moulded porcelain. First produced in 1908 and every year since. A cup and saucer with same pattern as the plate was introduced in 1980.*

133 *Madonna and Child*, 1908.
134 *The Shepherds*, 1918.
135 *In the Park*, 1919.
136 *Mary with the Child Jesus*, 1920.
137 *Three Singing Angels*, 1922.
138 *Christmas Star over the Sea*, 1924.
139 *Fishing Boats*, 1930.
140 *Mother and Child*, 1931.
141 *The Hermitage Castle*, 1934.
142 *Expeditionary Ship in Greenland Ice*, 1939.
143 *Amalienborg Palace*, 1954.
144 *Fetching the Christmas Tree*, 1964.
145 *The Last Umiak*, 1968.
146 *Christmas Rose and Cat*, 1970.
147 *In the Desert*, 1972.
148 *Winter Twilight*, 1974.
149 *Choosing a Christmas Tree*, 1979.
150 *Admiring the Christmas Tree*, 1981.

THE MODERN FACTORY

ROYAL COPENHAGEN

151

152

153

151-155 Porcelain figures by Christian Thomsen, 1898-1921. *Still in production.*

151 *Princess and Swineherd.*
152 *Peasant Women Gossiping.*
153 *Boy with Calf.*
154 *Girl with Calf.*
155 *Goose Girl.*

ROYAL COPENHAGEN

THE MODERN FACTORY

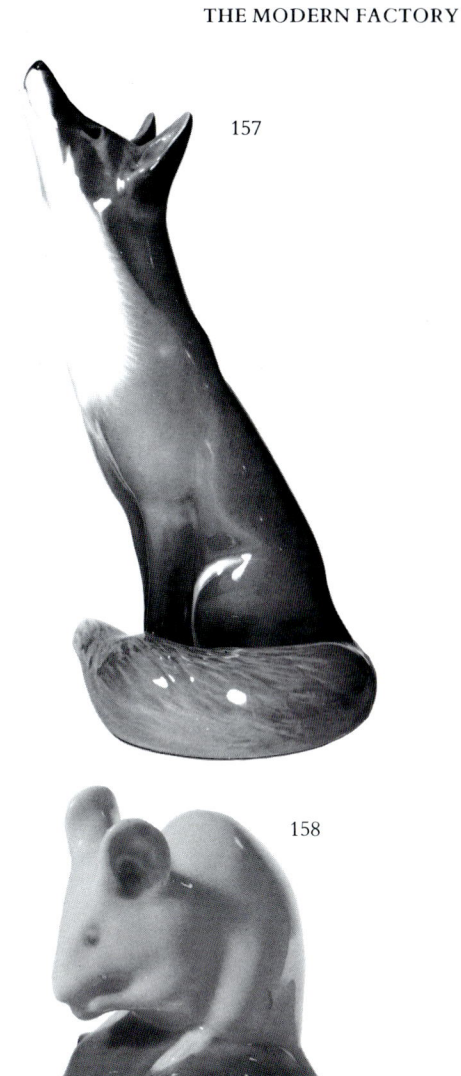

156

157

158

156-162 Studies from Nature, 1901-63. *Still in production.*
156 *Blue Fish (Coelacanth) by Jeanne Grut. Earthenware body, blue glaze. First made 1963. Length approx. 45in (1143mm).*
157 *Fox Barking. Porcelain, modelled by Erik Nielsen, 1910. Underglaze decorated. Victoria and Albert Museum, London.*
158 *Mouse on Cheese. Porcelain, modelled by Erik Nielsen, 1912. Underglaze decorated.*

159 *Barn Owls. Porcelain, modelled by Arnold Krog, 1901. Underglaze decorated.*

160 *Amherst Pheasants by Andrea Nielsen, 1907-17. Underglaze decorated.*

THE MODERN FACTORY

161 *Snowy Owl* (left) *and Long-Eared Owl. Modelled by Peter Herold 1917 and 1912 respectively. Underglaze decorated.*

162 *Kingfishers by Peter Herold, 1915-22. Underglaze decorated.*

APPENDIX A
The Artists and their Marks

Artists of the Mueller Period, 1775-1801, with approximate dates of engagement at the factory.

Abildgaard, Søren Pedersen, 1780-? Artistic consultant.
Arent, Johan. 1777-1788. Painter.

Bau, N. 1788-1820. Landscape painter, figure decorator. Silhouettes.
Bayer, Johan Christoph. 1776-1804. Painter, renowned for botanical painting on Flora Danica service.

Cadewitz, Martin. 1780-1791. Painter.
Camradt, F. C. 1780-1796. Portrait painter.
Camradt, J. L. 1794-1797. Flower and fruit painter.
Clio, Hans. 1775-1785. Painter and factory drawing master.

Faxoe, Nicolai Christian. 1776-1810. Flower painter.

Hald, Andreas. 1781-1797. Modeller and sculptor.
Hansen, Lars. 1775-1800. Painter. Specialist in blue underglaze decoration.
Holm, J. J. 1780-1816. Modeller and sculptor.

Jensen, Chr. A., c. 1780-? Painter.

Kalleberg, G. 1779-1811. Modeller (chiefly figures) and repoussé worker.

Lehmann, Peter Heinrich. 1780-1800. Berliner. Painter.
Luplau, Anton Carl. 1776-1795. Modelmaster. Trained at Fürstenberg.

Meehl, Hans. c. 1790. Modeller.
Meyer, Elias. 1780-1792. Painter. Trained at Dresden.
Meyer, M. 1784-1792. Painter.

Ondrup, Hans Christoph. 1778-1814. Painter.

Preus, Soren. 1784-? Modeller. Exceptional floral work.

Schmidt, Jacob. 1778-1807. Modeller and sculptor.
Svardalyn, Raben. 1779-1814. Painter. Specialist in underglaze blue.

Thomaschevsky, Carl F. 1780-? Berliner, arrived with Lehmann but left after short while. Painter.
Tvede, Claus. 1775-1783. Sculptor and modeller.

Principal artists of the nineteenth and twentieth centuries, with dates of birth and death where available

Andersen, Mogens. Born 1916. Has designed stoneware vases and bowls for the factory.

Bøgelund, Gerd. Born 1923. Ceramist. At factory from 1946.
Buch, Bodil. Born 1945. Ceramist.

Engelhardt, Valdemar. 1860-1915. Chemist. Specialist in crystalline glazes. At factory from 1892.

Fischer, V. T. At factory 1894-1928. Painter of animal subjects.

Grut, Jeanne. Born 1927. Sculptor and modeller. At factory from 1959.

Halier, Carl. 1873-1948. Ceramist. At factory from 1913-48.
Hallin, F. A. 1865-1947. Painter. At factory 1885-1895.

Hansen, Bente. Born 1943. Ceramist.
Hansen-Reistrup, 1863-1929. Painter.
Hetsch, G. F. 1788-1864. Architect. Artistic adviser 1828-64.
Høst, Marianne. 1865-1943. Painter. At factory 1885-1904.

Jensen, Oluf. 1871-1934. Painter. At factory from 1885-1934.

Klein, C. L. 1810-1891. Painter. At factory from 1825-1891.
Kock, Vilhelm. 1809-1865. Painter. At factory 1842-51.
Krog, Arnold. 1856-1931. Architect and painter. Artistic Director 1885-1916, then artistic adviser to 1931.
Kyhn, Knud. 1880-1969. Sculptor and painter. Specialised in stoneware animal figures. At factory 1903-67.

Lange, Kaj. Born 1905. Designer. At factory from 1934.
Liisberg, C. F. 1860-1909. Sculptor and painter. At factory 1885-1909.
Lundberg, Theodor. 1852-1926. Swedish sculptor.
Lyngbye, L. R. 1809-1963. Painter.

Madsen, Theodor. 1880-1965. Sculptor and modeller. At factory 1896-1935.
Malmer, Ellen. Born 1942. Ceramist. At factory from 1965.
Meyer, Grethe. Born 1918. Designer.
Mortensen, C. 1861-1945. Painter. At factory 1887-1901.

Nielsen, Erik. 1857-1947. Sculptor and figure modeller. At factory 1887-1926.
Nielsen, Jais. 1885-1961. Painter and sculptor. At factory from 1921.
Nordström, Patrick. 1870-1929. Ceramist. Specialist in stoneware. At factory 1912-22.

Olrik, O. H. B. 1830-90. Sculptor.
Olsen, Thorkild. 1890-1973. Painter and ceramist. At factory 1908-1968.
Orth, Emil. 1833-1919. Painter. At factory 1869-1902.

Petersen, Gerd Hiort. Born 1937. Ceramist. At factory 1965-1973.

Rode, Gotfred. 1862-1937. Painter. At factory from 1896-1933.

Salto, Axel. 1889-1961. Painter, sculptor and ceramist. At factory from 1930.
Slott-Møller, Harold. 1864-1937. Painter.
Staehr-Nielsen, Eva. 1911-1976. Ceramist. At factory 1968-1976.
Stephensen, Snorre. Born 1943. Ceramist.
Svardalyn, J. Painter. At factory 1808-1838.

Thomsen, Christian. 1860-1921. Sculptor and modeller. At factory 1898-1920.
Thorsson, Nils. 1898-1982. Ceramist. At factory 1912-1975.
Trolle, Anne-Marie. Born 1944. Ceramist.

Weiss, Ivan. Born 1946. Ceramist.

ROYAL COPENHAGEN

Painters' Marks
1-2. Blue-painter marks, 1775-1814; 3-4. Blue-painter marks, 1863-1931; 5. Letter-mark on blue painted porcelain, 1931—; 6. Fraction-marking (see note), 1894–; 7. Valdemar Engelhardt, F = yearmark, each letter with numbers 1-1000; 8. Arnold Krog, 1884-1916, 3 = March, D = 1888; 9. Christian Thomsen, 1898-1921; 10. Vilhelm Kock, 1842-51; 11. C. L. Klein, 1825-91; 12. Emil Orth, 1869-1902; 13. F. A. Hallin, 1885-95; 14. Gotfred Rode, 1896-1933; 15. Marianne Høst, 1885-1904; 16. C. F. Liisberg, 1885-1909; 17. Theodor Madsen, 1900-35; 18. Patrick Nordström, 1912-22; 19. Carl Halier, 1913-48; 20. Knud Kyhn, 1903-67; 21. Jais Nielsen, 1921-61; 22. Axel Salto, 1930-61; 23. Nils Thorsson, 1918–; 24. Thorkild Olsen, 1908-68; 25. Kaj Lange, 1934–; 26. Gerd Bogelund, 1946–; 27. Eva Stæhr-Nielsen, 1968–; 28. Jeanne Grut, 1959–; 29. Ellen Malmer, 1965–; 30. Mogens Anderson, 1970–.

THE ARTISTS AND THEIR MARKS

Blue-painter Marks
Some early marks on blue wares cannot be identified for artist or period. However the marks illustrated above appear on blue wares.
The first blue-painter's mark with two digits appeared in 1863; marks 20-30 in 1875; 30-40 in 1885. The marks were, however, passed from one artist to another.

Lars Hansen?

1894-   **A. Lassen 1853-77**   **1966**   **1966**

Note: Fraction codes were introduced in 1894. The number above the stroke indicates the number of the decoration (not the decorator), and the number below represents the item.
Thus $\frac{10}{1626}$ *(above)* can be decoded as 'decoration no. 10 on item no. 1626'.

J. C. Bayer

151

APPENDIX B
The Clays

The Clays
Early recipes

Kaolin from the Bornholm deposits in Denmark was used from 1775 until 1881 when it was discontinued altogether. From the earliest days of the Royal Manufactory, however, clays from the St. Yrieix deposits in France were used in varying quantities up to the present century when Cornish clay (kaolin) became the principal ingredient. The very pure French clay was imported first in the year 1778 (four barrels) and was used increasingly until 1792 when the Revolution and the European coalition against France prevented further deliveries. Deliveries resumed in quantity in 1805 (58 barrels against 187 in 1792) but were again cut off in 1807 when Britain declared war on Denmark and blockaded its waters. By 1812 the French kaolin, which had been used sparingly for mixing with native clay and for the finest wares, was exhausted and the factory was forced to revert to the Bornholm clays. Thus there was a brief period of three years, 1812-15, when the Copenhagen wares exhibited a distinctly grey and uneven body appearance. The method of dry purification with powerful magnets was insufficient to remove all the iron particles, and mica proved another inseparable impurity. In 1815 the factory perfected the washing method which enabled it to produce a pure white porcelain from the Bornholm kaolin and china stone. In 1817 the then administrator, Peter Garlieb, was able to decline an offer of Limoges clay, although he had second thoughts and ordered a quantity soon afterwards during a journey in France. Eighteen barrels remained in the warehouse ten years later, so successful was the 'washed' Bornholm clay, and it was not until 1843 that regular deliveries from Limoges were resumed for use in a newly constituted paste containing Bornholm and French clay (with quartz of course) for bisquewares.

In 1859 another bisqueware paste was introduced, using French kaolin only. A mix containing Bornholm kaolin only was used until 1881 for the blue-painted wares. In the years just prior to World War II Czechoslovak kaolin was imported by the factory, but for most of the present century Cornish kaolin has been the staple diet.

The Mueller clays

Mueller originally composed three recipes, only the first of which continued to be used after 1779.

	No.I %	No.II %	No.III %
Bornholm kaolin	37.5	69.2	39.2
Feldspar	8.3	15.4	13.1
Quartz	54.2	15.4	47.7

From 1779 the factory used three pastes, No.I above and:

	No.II 'Danish Clay' %	No.III 'Virgin Clay' %
Bornholm kaolin	13.8	–
Quartz	22.3	–
Feldspar	26.6	25.8
French kaolin	37.3	74.2

In 1794 Mueller introduced Clay No.IV which was used increasingly from the following year:

	No.IV %
Bornholm kaolin	12.3
Quartz	18.9
Feldspar	25.5
French kaolin	43.3

'Danish clay' was the prevalent paste until 1794 but was rapidly succeeded by No.IV and was discontinued in 1803. 'Virgin clay', the whitest of the mixes, was used only for the most luxurious items such as gilded and elaborately decorated dinnerware and expensive gift articles. Its pure, quartz-free body was difficult to support in the kiln and demanded the highest glost-fire in order to achieve vitrification.

The Mueller Glazes

In 1774* Mueller published details of his three original glaze recipes, as follows:

No.1
White clay
Chalk   of each VI pounds
Sand   of each XII pounds
Feldspar   of each XX pounds

No.2
White clay
Chalk   of each VI pounds
Sand   of each XII pounds
Feldspar   of each XXIV pounds

No.3
White clay
Chalk   of each VI pounds
Feldspar   of each XXIV pounds
Sand   of each XII pounds
Fluorspar   of each III pounds

*Probably as part of a prospectus to shareholders.

These formulae were abandoned in 1779 when a single glaze was devised for the 'Danish' and 'Virgin' clay bodies. In 1794 Mueller composed a glaze for No.IV clay. Both contained a higher proportion of quartz than his earlier recipes. A third glaze was developed, known as 'Besserweiss', for repairing on-glaze decorated wares which were fired in the muffle-kiln after re-glazing.

APPENDIX C
The Factory Marks

FACTORY MARKS
1. 1775-1820 and c. 1850-70; 2. 1820-50; 3. 1870-90; 4. 1889; 5. c. 1892; 6. 1894-1900; 7. 1894-1922; 8. 1905-, so-called Juliane Marie mark; 9. 1922-; 10. c. 1923; 11. 1929-50, used on so-called 'matte porcelain' only; 12. c. 1863, on earthenware; 13. 1868-1922, on earthenware; 14. 1872-1930, on earthenware, best quality; 15. 1903-69 on earthenware with many-coloured decorations under glaze; 16. Copyright on biscuit, 1835-.

Select Bibliography

Some publications are shown in duplicate under separate headings for ease of reference.

Andersen, Johannes (Ed), *Teknik, keramisk Kunst,* Møller, 1946.

Bech, E., *The Royal Copenhagen Porcelain Company Ltd,* London, 1935.

Belshaw, J. S., 'Copenhagen Blue and Otherwise', excerpt from *The Antiquarian,* April 1928.

Bodelsen, Merete, *Gauguin's Ceramics,* Faber and Faber, 1964; *Patrick Nordström 1870-1929,* Copenhagen, 1956. See also *Porslin, Dansk keramik,* and *Royal Copenhagen Porcelain Manufactory 1775-1975.*

Christensen, Victor P., 'Danish Porcelain in the 18th Century', excerpt from the *Connoisseur,* August 1923; *Den kgl. danske Porcelainsfabrik i 18 Aarhundrede, Bordservicer og Figurer* (series *Kunst i Danmark*), Copenhagen, 1938.

Copenhagen, *The Royal Porcelain Manufactory 1775-1975,* Copenhagen, 1975; *Fifty Years in Old Bond Street,* London, 1951; *200 Years of Royal Copenhagen,* catalogue of retrospective exhibition circulated by The Smithsonian Institution, 1974-76, Copenhagen, 1976.

Danske Kunstindustrimuseum, *Dansk Porselan 1760-1800,* Copenhagen, 1933.

Dansk keramik: articles by **Grandjean, Bodelsen and others,** Stockholm, 1960. Also published as *Porslin;* see under.

David, C. L. (the C. L. David Collection), *Samling Nogle Studier,* 2 vols, Copenhagen, 1948; *Dansk Kunst,* Copenhagen, 1972.

Dusseldorf – Museum Hetjens, *Dänische Keramik, Arbeiten der Königlischen Porzellan Manufaktur Kopenhagen aus Gegegwart und Vergangenheit,* Dusseldorf, 1970.

Frohme, J. W., *Danske fajancer; historiske meddelelser om fajancefabriker i Danmark og hertugdommerne i det 18.aarhundrede* (facsimiles of marks), Copenhagen, 1911.

Giacomotti, Jeanne, *La Céramique 111 – la faience fine et la porcelaine,* Paris, 1964 (reprint)

Grandjean, Bredo L., *Konelig dansk Porcelain, 1775-1884,* Copenhagen, 1948; revised edition of foregoing with photos, marks etc., Copenhagen, 1962; *Dansk ostindisk porcelaen importen fra Kanton ca.1700-1822,* Copenhagen, 1965; *The Flora Danica Service,* Copenhagen, 1973; *Det Musselmalede Stel,* Copenhagen, 1950; *Blaablomstrede Stel,* Copenhagen, 1968; *Biscuit efter Thorvaldsen,* Thorvaldsen Museum, 1978; 'Ferdinand – Charles Muller à Copenhagne', excerpt from *Faenza,* XLVIII, nos. 1-2, 1962; *Nils Thorsson,* Copenhagen, 1952; 'Nogle nyer hvervelsen af dansk porcelaen', excerpt from *Journal of the Danish Museum of Decorative Art,* 1964; 'La Collection d'étranger à la bibliothèque de la Manufacture Royal de Porcelaine de Copenhagne', excerpt from *Faenza,* Anno XLVI, no.1, 1960; *Den kongelige danske Porcelaensfabriks . . . indtil ca.1800,* Arv og Eje, 1958; See also *Porslin, Dansk keramik* and *Royal Copenhagen Porcelain Manufactory 1775-1975.*

Hannover, Emil, *Keramisk Haandbog,* Copenhagen, 1924.

Hayden, Arthur, *Chats on Royal Copenhagen Porcelain,* T. Fisher Unwin, 1918.

Hiort, Esbjorn, *Moderne dansk keramik,* Copenhagen, 1955.

Krog, Arnold, (75th birthday tribute) in *Nyt Tidsskrift for Kunstindustri,* vol.4, no.3, March 1931.

Lassen, Erik, *En kobenhavnsk porcelaensfabrikshistorie – Bing & Grondahl 1853-1978,* Copenhagen, 1978.

Myers, Lucien, '200 Years of Copenhagen', from *Tableware International,* June 1975.

Nielsen, K., *Danske, norske og svenske keramiske marker; forsog til en vejledning for samlere af K.N.* (with facsimiles of marks), Copenhagen, 1948.

Nyrop, Camillus, *Danske Fajence og Porcellainsmaerker,* Copenhagen, 1881.

Oigaard, A., *Fajencefabriken i Store Kongensgade,* Copenhagen, 1936; 'The Copenhagen Faience Factory 1722-1772', excerpt from *Old Furniture,* vol.V, November 1928.

Philippovich, Eugen von, 'Zwei Porzellanmedaillons im Schweizerischen Landesmuseum, Zurich', *Keramik-Freunde der Schweiz,* no.44, October 1958.

Paris: Exhibition catalogue, Musée des Arts Decoratifs, *Formes Scandinares,* November 1958-January 1959.

Porslin no. 5-6, *Dansk Keramik* a special number edited by **Bredo L. Grandjean** with articles – 'Det Danske Underglasurmaleri' by **Sigurd Schultz,** 'Dekorative Arbejder i Porcelaen' by **Grandjean and Dyveke Helsted,** 'Tradition og Stilskifte i Dansk Stentoj' by **Merete Bodelsen,** 'Dansk Lertoj i Dagby' by **Lars Thirslund,** and 'Bordserviser' by **Gunnar Jespersen.** Stockholm, 1960. Also published as *Dansk Keramik,* Stockholm, 1960.

Reuter, E., 'Old Copenhagen Porcelain', article in *Connoisseur,* vol. XIII, 1905.

Royal Copenhagen Porcelain Manufactory 1775-1975, commemorative book published to mark 200th anniversary of factory, with articles – 'The Royal Factory' by **Bredo L. Grandjean,** 'Arnold Krog and his Porcelain' by **Dyveke Helsted,** and 'Sèvres-Copenhagen; Crystal Glazes and Stoneware at the Turn of the Century' by **Merete Bodelsen.** Copenhagen, 1975.

Udall, Kai, *Gammel dansk fajence fra fabriker i kongeriget og hertugdommerne,* Copenhagen, 1961. New edition 1967.

Winstone, Victor (H.V.F.), 'Two Centuries of Royal Copenhagen', article in *Connoisseur,* June 1975.

General Pottery

Berling, Karl, *Das Meissner Porzellan,* Leipzig, 1900.

Bindman, David (Ed), 'Flaxman and New-Classicism', *Catalogue of Royal Academy of Arts,* for Exhibition in London, 26 Oct-9 Dec 1979.

Borrmann, H., *Moderne Keramik,* Berlin, 1902.

Eyles, Desmond, *Royal Doulton 1815-1965,* Hutchinson, 1965.

Garner, Sir Harry, *Oriental Blue and White,* Faber and Faber, 1954.

Hillier, Bevis, *Pottery and Porcelain 1700-1914* (in the *Social History of the Decorative Arts* series), Weidenfeld and Nicolson, 1968.

Hofmann, Fr. H., *Das Porzellan der Europaischen Manufacturen im 18. Jahrhundert,* Berlin, 1932.

Honey, W. B., *French Porcelain,* Faber and Faber, 1950; *German Porcelain,* Faber and Faber, 1947.

Jenyns, Soame, *Later Chinese Porcelain,* Faber and Faber, 1951; *Japanese Pottery,* Faber and Faber, 1971.

Mankowitz, Wolf, *Wedgwood,* Spring Books, 1953.

Watney, Bernard, *English Blue and White of the Eighteenth Century,* Faber and Faber, 1963.

Wedgwood, Josiah C., *Staffordshire Pottery and its History,* Sampson Low, 1913.

Whiter, Leonard, *Spode,* Barrie & Jenkins, 1970.

Background

Miles, R., *Candles in Denmark,* John Murray, 1958.

Piles, Comte de A.-T.-J.-A.-M.-M. Fortia de (with M.-L. de Boisgelin de Kerdu), *Voyage de deux Francais en Allemagne, Danemarck, Suede, Russie et Pologne, fait en 1790-1792,* Paris, Desenne, 1796 (5 vols).

Wilkins, W. H., *A Queen of Tears, Caroline Matilda, Queen of Denmark and Norway, and Princess of Great Britain and Ireland,* London, 1904.

Index

In this Index the letter 'c' denotes a caption; 'n' a note; 'a' an Appendix. All numbers refer to page numbers.

A

Abildgaard, Nicolai, 24, 148a
Aesthetic movement, 87
Ahrensborg, Christian, 24
Alcocks, Staffordshire, 84
Alexandra, Queen of England, 50, 93
Altonaischer Mercurius, quoted, 39
Aluminia factory, 63, 86, 112
Amalienborg Palace, 48, 49
American War of Independence, bowl, 29
Amstel pottery, 60
Andersen, Hans, 94, 121
Andersen, Mogens, 110, 124, 149a
Antvorskov pottery, 63
Antwerp, 89
Arabia, 61
Arabian Nights, 121
Arent, Johan, 148a
Art décoratif, 118
Art et Décoration, 110
Art Faience, range, 112-113, 124
Artist, The, 10
Artists and marks 148a
Art nouveau, 87, 103, 118
Arts and crafts movement, 21
Assyria, 10
Auclair, L., 110
Aue, clay deposits, 13
August(us) II, Elector of Saxony and King of Poland, 13
Auliczek, Dominicus, 46

B

Baca range, 124
Babylonia, 10
Bartolozzi, Fr., 41n
Bau, N., 24, 148a
Bauhaus, philosophy, 116
Bayer, Johan Christoph, 24, 26, 46, 48, 67, 93, 148a
Beardsley, Aubrey, 87
Beerbohm, Max, 87
Beethoven, Ludwig van, 84
Bentley, Thomas, 31n, 44n
Berling, Karl, 58
Berlin Porcelain Manufactory, 14, 17, 74, 80, 84, 85, 103, 115
Bernini, Giovanni, 21
Bethevin, Pierre, 14n
Bindesbøll, Gottlieb, 118
Bindesbøll, Thorvald, 118
Bing and Grondahl Porcelain Manufactory, 63
Bing, Samuel, 90, 96, 116
Blaublumchen, see Blue Flowers

Bloch, Kresten, 110
Blondeau, Vincennes modeller, 80
Blue and White, decoration, 56-71; Muhammadan blue, 60
'Blue Fish', 131
Blue Flowers, 11, 56, 64-71, 121
'Blue Fluted' pattern, 57-64, 89, 121; 'Immortelle' and 'Copenhagen' descriptions, 58ff, 60, 64, 89
'Blue Line' service, 132
Blue Tower factory, 14, 17
Blyt, Johan Koren, 65
Bodelsen, Merete, 96n, 98n, 100n
Boettger, Johann Friedrich, 13, 14
Bøgelund, Gerd, 110, 124, 149a
Boisgelin, Chevalier Louis de, 21, 42, 46
Bone china, 84
Bornholm clays, 14n, 31, 66, 107, 109, 152a
Borrmann, H., 118
Boston Museum, 96n
Botanical Garden, Copenhagen, 48
'Boy with Calf', figure, 94
Brandenstein pattern (German), 65
Brooks, Mr, 100
Bruehl, Count Heinrich von, 21, 51
Bryant, Jacob, 41n
Buch, Bodil, 149a
Budapest, auction, 50
Buen Retiro (Capodimonte), see Madrid
Bulletin Chimique, 98
Bülow, Johan, 46, 49
Burne-Jones, Sir Edward, 87
Burton, William, 13n, 105n, quoted 114
Bushell, S. W., 61n
Bustelli, Franz Anton, 15, 21, 80
Byron, George Gordon, Lord, 84

C

Cadewitz, Martin, 148a
Camradt, F. C., 24, 33, 148a
Camradt, J. L., 24, 148a
Canada, 15
'Capella' service, 134
Caroline Matilde, Queen of Denmark, 18
Carriès, Jean, 110
Catherine II, Empress of Russia, 44, 46
Caughley Porcelain Manufactory, 57n, 60
Cazin, Michel, 105
Chantilly pottery, 15n
Chaplet, Ernest, 98, 100, 105, 109
Charles I, Duke of Brunswick, 15, 19
Charles XV, King of Sweden, 50
Chien wares, 104
China, ceramics of, 10, 12, 13, 56, 61, 89, 90, 116
Ch'ing dynasty wares, 57

Ching-tê-chên, kilns of, 12
Chinoiserie, 57, 121
Christian VII, King of Denmark (1766-1808), 15, 17, 18, 20; portrait on vase 24, 26, 46, 48, 49
Christian VIII, King of Denmark (1839-48), 49
Christian IX, King of Denmark, 50
Christiansborg Palace, 21, 28, 30ff, 42, 48, 49, 85
Christensen, Victor P., 51n
Christmas plates (annual), 134
Cipriani, G. B., 41n
Clausen, Finn, 28
Clays, factory recipes 1775-1881, 152-3a
Clio, Hans, 24, 148a
Clemens, J. F., 33
Clément, Adolphe, 64, 89, 90, 96ff
Coalport, 121
Cobalt, see Blue and White
Coloured glazes, see Crystalline glazes
Commemorative wares, 26c, 29, 134
Copenhagen, *passim*; and Battle of, 26ff, 134; bowl in commemoration of, 29
Copehagen Gazette, 20
'Copenhagen' pattern, see Blue and White
Copenhagen, Royal Porcelain Manufactory, *passim*; and attitude to ceramics, 13; foundation of Kobmagergade establishment and adoption of factory mark, 16ff; ownership by Christian VII and adoption of name Den Kongelige Danske Porcelains Fabrik, 19; retail shop, 20; move to Frederiksborg (1844), 50, 87; importance of blue decoration, 57; revival under Krog's direction 86ff; amalgamation with Aluminia Company (1884), 86, 112
Cornish Clay, 152a
Creamware (Wedgwood), 84
Crystalline glazes, 98-103
Cyfflé, Paul-Louis, 76
Czechoslovak clays, 152a

D

Dalgas, Frederick, 109, 112
Dalpayrat, Adrien, 98, 105
Dansk Folke Museum, captions *passim*
Dammouse, A., 105
David, C. L., 67n
Deck, Théodore, 105n
Delaherche, Auguste, 98, 109
Delft pottery, 10, 56, 57, 112
Denmark, *passim*
Derby (later Royal Crown Derby), 121

157

Deutsche Blumen, see Blue Flowers
'Diana' range, 131
Dingwall, Colonel K., 67n
Doat, Taxile, 103, 110
Doccia Porcelain Manufactory, 31
Domino service, 134
Doulton, Sir Henry, 104
Dresden, see Meissen
Duquesnoy, Francois (Il Fiammingo), 21
Dutailly, 98
Dwight, John, 13

E

East India Companies, 12, 42
Edward VII, King of England, 50
Edwards, William, 86n
Eickstedt, General, 18
Elers, D. and J., 13
Elsinore, see Kronborg
Empire style, 85
Enamel decoration, 43
Encyclopaedia Britannica, 114
Engelhardt, Valdemar, 94, 100ff, 107, 149a
Entrecolles, Père d', 61
'Europa', figure, 72
Evans, William, 68n
Evelyn, John, 21n
Exhibitions: Paris Exposition (1867), 104, 115; Chaplet display, Paris (1887), 98; Industry, Agriculture and Art (with Japanese section), Copenhagen (1888), 90; Paris (1889), 90; Chicago World Fair (1893), 100; Paris (1900), 103, 104; Danish Society of Arts and Crafts (1912), 109
Eyles, Desmond, 98n, 100n, 105n

F

Fabricius, Dr F. V. P., 46
Factory marks, 154a
Faenza, 112
Faience, 112
Falck, A., 85
Fama figures, 39, 41
Famille rose, 58n
Famille verte, 58n
Fan service, 94
Faxoe, Nicolai Christian, 24, 48, 148a
Felspar (feldspar or china stone), 13, 14c
'Fels and Vogel', Meissen pattern, 67
Figures, 72-83
Fischer, O. (dedication), 26
Fischer, V. Th., 92n, 149a
Flambé glazes, 98; see also Crystalline glazes
'Flamed' glazes, see Crystalline glazes
Flaxman, John, 31n, 41n

Flora Danica, 11, 26, 44-55, 65, 121; Princess Alexandra version, 50, 56
Florence (Medici) wares, 13
'Flow' glazes (*coulées*), see Crystalline glazes
Forrest, Mr, 100
Fournier, Louis, 14, 15, 31
Fragonard, Jean Honoré, 21
France, ceramics of, 13, 57
Franco-Prussian War, 84
Fransiscan Pottery (USA), 63
Fredensborg Palace, 35
Frederick II, King of Prussia, 15
Frederik V, King of Denmark (1746-66), 14, 15, 17, 61
Frederik VI, King of Denmark (1808-39); as Crown Prince, 18, 26, 29, 30ff, 46
Frederik, Heir Presumptive to Danish throne, 18, 19, 26, 30, 72
Frederik VII, King of Denmark, 50
Frederiksborg, 50, 76n, 87
French Revolution, 84
Frijsenborg service, 134
Fulham Pottery, 13
Furnival Pottery, 63
Fürstenberg Porcelain Manufactory, 15, 17, 19, 33, 37, 67, 72, 74

G

Gallé, Emile, 91, 98
Garlieb, Peter, 152a
Garner, Sir Harry, 57n, 61n, 67n
Garnier, Edouard, 91, 100, 103
Gauguin, Paul, 96
Gazette des Beaux-Arts, 91
George III, King of England, 18
Gibbon, Edward, 61
Gladding and McBean, see Fransiscan
Goethe, Johann Wolfgang von, 84
'Goose Girl', figure, 94
Gothic revival, 89
Grandjean, Bredo L., quoted 12, 19, 35, 60ff, and in notes throughout
Griegst, Arje, 134
Grönland, Peter, 27, 48
Grossi, Luigi, 72
Grund, J. G., 83c
Grut, Jeanne, 124, 149a
Guldberg, Ove Hoegh, 18
'Gundestrup' glaze, 124
Gustavsberg Pottery, 63

H

Hald, Andreas, 29, 148a
Halier, Carl, 110, 124, 149a
Hallin, F. A., 63, 92n, 149a

Hamburg Museum für Kunst und Gewerbe, 50
Hamilton, Lady, 27
Hamilton, Sir William, 31
Hannover, Emil, 47n, 58n, 60, 98
Hansen, Bente, 124, 149a
Hansen, C. F., 42
Hansen, Hans Jacob, 24
Hansen, Lars, 67, 148a
Hansen-Reistrup, 149a
Harboe, R., 112
Harsdorff, 35
Hassø, A. G., 49n
Hauch, 48
Hayden, Arthur, 10, 44, 74, and in notes throughout
Helsted, Dyveke, 87n, 90n, 96n, 118n
Henning, Gerhard, 94, 121
Hennings, August, 19
Hetsch, G. G., 68, 85, 149a
Hillier, Bevis, quoted 12; 13n, 14n, quoted 15, 118
Hirschsprung, Bernard, 96, 98
Hjorth, Hans, 109
Hoechst Porcelain Manufactory, 74
Hoentschel, Georges, 105
Hofmann, Fr. H., 51
Hokusai, 90, 118
Holland, ceramics of, 57
Holm, F. E., 50n
Holm, Jesper Johansen, 24, 79, 148a
Holm, Theodor (Holmskjold), 18, 19, 24, 26, 27, 35, 44, 46, 48
Honey, W. B., 13n, 50n, 96n
Høst, Marianne, 149a
Huet, C., 31

I

Ilmenau Pottery, 60
Ilssing, Stephen, 92n
'Immortelle' decoration. See Blue Fluted.
India, 15
Industrial Revolution, 84, 87
Islam, 61

J

Japan, 90, 96, 115ff
Japonisme, 90
Jardin, N.-H., 49
Jeanneney, Paul, 105
Jensen, Chr. A., 46
Jensen, Georg, 134
Jensen, Helge, 110
Jensen, Oluf, 64, 90, 94, 149a
Jenyns, Soame, 96n

INDEX

Joachim, Christian, 112, 124, 132
Juel, Andreas, 68
Juel, Jens, 33
Juliane Marie, Queen of Denmark (1752-66); as Dowager Queen, 12, 15ff, 27, 30ff; Luplau's bust of, 72; Stanley's bust of, frontispiece; so-called mark of (1905), 94

K

Kaendler, Johann Joachim, 15, 21, 51, 80
Kähler, Herman, 118
Kalleberg, G., 24, 72, 79, 148a
Kaolin, 13, 152a; see also Bornholm
Kashan wares, 57, 68
Klein, Adalbert, 103n
Klein, C. L., 149a
Klipfel, C. J. C., 64
Kock, Vilhelm, 149a
Krog, Arnold, 50, 51, 60, 64, 66, 86-95, 98, 107, 109, 134, 149a
Krohn, Pietro, 79n, 92n
Kronborg (Elsinore), 28, 85
Kublai Khan, 12
Kyhn, Knud, 107, 110, 124, 149a
Kunstindustrimuseum, Copenhagen, 79 and in notes and captions throughout

L

Lachenal, Edmont, 98
Lambeth art school, 104
Landsretten (High Court) action, 64
Lane, Arthur, 57n
Lange, Kaj, 149a
Langen, J. G. von, 15, 19
Lauth, 98
Lehmann, Peter Heinrich, 24, 148a
Lessore, Emile, 105n
Liisberg, C. F., 92n, 149a
Limoges clays, 152a
Lister, Dr Martin, 13n
Lorentzen, C. A., 27c
Louis XV, 14, 15
Louise Augusta, Princess, 33
Lowestoft Pottery, 60
Luecke, J. C. L. von, 14n
Lundberg, Theodor, 149a
Lunéville porcelain, 76
Luplau, A. C., 19, 24, 33, 37, 60, 72ff, 148a
Luplau, C. D., 43c
Lyngbye, L. R., 85, 149a

M

Madrid, 80
Madsen, Karl, 46n, 47n, 94n, 96
Madsen, Theodor, 94, 149a
Maiolica (tin-glazed earthenware), 10, 56, 57, 112
Malinowsky, Arno, 121
Malmer, Ellen, 124, 149a
Mankowitz, Wolf, 44n, 84n
Manthey, 48
Marieberg pottery, 14
Marguerite service, 92
Marlborough gem, 41
Marryat, Sir Horace, 50
Martin-Hansen, Carl, 121
Marx, Roget, 91
Massier, 98
McCarthy, Denis, 14
Meakin family, Staffordshire, 84
Medici wares, 13, 57n
Meehl, Hans, 79, 148a
Mehlhorn, Gottfried, 14n
Mehlhorn, Gottlieb, 14
Meissen Porcelain Manufactory, 13, 14, 15, 17, 21, 57, 58, 60, 65, 67, 74, 84, 94
Meissonnier, Juste-Aurèle, 21
Mennecy pottery, 14n
Mesopotamia, 57, 61
Meyer, Elias, 24, 148a
Meyer, F. E., 80
Meyer, Grethe, 149a
Meyer, M., 24, 148a
Michelsen, A., 134
Ming dynasty wares, 12, 57, 67
Minton, Thomas (and factory), 10, 57n, 84, 105n
Modum, Norway; cobalt deposits, 65
Mogensen, Jorgen, 110
Moltke, Count Adam Gottlob, 15, 17
Moltke Palace, 48
Monkhouse, C., 13n
Moore, George, 87
Morris, William, 21, 87
Morse, Edward Sylvester, 96
Mortensen, Carl, 118, 149a
Mozart, Wolfgang Amadeus, 15
Mueller, Anna Catherine, née Holm, 27
Mueller, Frantz Henrich, 16ff, 31, 37, 39, 42, 46ff, 57, 65, 80, 89, 90, 134; clays and glazes 153a
Muhammadan blue, see Blue and White
Museum of Mineralogy, Copenhagen, 98
Mussel-painted wares, see Blue Fluted

N

Napoleon Bonaparte, 84
Napoleonic Wars, 26, 84
National Museum, Stockholm, 50n, 79
Nelson, Admiral Lord, 27
Neo-classical art, 35, 84
New Hall Porcelain Manufactory, 60
Niebuhr, Carsten, 61
Nielsen, Erik, 94, 124, 149a
Nielsen, Frederik M., 94
Nielsen, Jais, 110, 149a
Ninagawa Noritani, 96
Ninsei (Nomomura Seibei), 96
Niss, Thorvald, 87
Nordström, Patrick, 109, 124, 149a
Norway, dual monarchy, 50
Nymphenburg Porcelain Manufactory, 15, 21, 46, 74, 80
Nyon pottery, 60
Nyrop, C., 86n

O

Oeder, G. Chr., 46
Ogier, Jean-Francois, quoted 15
Oland pottery, 63
Olrik, O. H. B., 149a
Olsen, Benjamin, 92n
Olsen, Thorkild, 149a
Ondrup, Hans Christoph, 24, 31, 33, 148a
Orth, Emil, 149a
Ozier patterns, 65, 94

P

Pater, Walter, 87
Pâte tendre, see Soft-paste
Pergolesi, M. A., 41n
Persia (Iran), 57, 61, 68
Petersen, Gerd Hiort, 124, 149a
Petuntse, see Felspar
Phillips, J. G., quoted 12
Piles, Comte Fortia de, 21, 42, 46, 47
Pipes, smoking, 134
Plessen, Mme de, 18
Polo, Marco and family, 12
Porcelain, hard-paste 13ff and *passim*
Porcelaine nouvelle, see Sèvres
Porsgrund pottery, 63
Pre-Raphaelite Movement, 87
Preus, Soren, 24, 47, 148a
'Princess on the Pea', figure, 94
'Princess and Swineherd', figure, 94

Q

'Queensware' (Creamware), see Wedgwood

R

Rackham, Bernard, quoted 94

Redwares, 13
Revue des Arts Décoratifs, 92
Richter, Johann Georg, 17
Ridinger, J. E., 31
Riedel, G.-F., 31
Rode, G., 92n, 149a
Roepsdorff, U. W. de, 26c
Rörstrand pottery, 60, 63
Rosenborg Palace, 14, 31ff, 49ff
Rosenkrantz, Niels, 44
Round Tower, Copenhagen, 27
Royal Academy, Copenhagen, 76
Ruskin, John, 87

S

Saint Cloud, 13
Saint Yrieix, clay deposits, 31, 66, 152a
Salmonsen, William, 90, 98
Salto, Axel, 100, 124, 149a
Saly, Jacques-Francois-Joseph, 35, 76
'San Ildefonso Faun', 76, 80
Saxony, cobalt ores from, 65; and see Meissen
Schack Palace, 48n
Schiott, August, 86n
Schimmelmann, Count, 48
Schlegel, Abraham, 65
Schlossmuseum, Berlin, 50
Schmidt, Jacob, 24, 79, 148a
Schou, Philip, 86, 87, 109
Schubert, Franz, 84
Seven Years' War, 15
Sèvres Porcelain Manufactory, 10, 14, 15, 77, 89, 91, 96, 98, 100, 103ff, 110, 115
Shaw, Simeon, 13n, 68n, 84n
Slott-Møller, Harold, 112, 149a
Soft-paste porcelain, 13ff
Soldani-Benzi, Massimiliano, 31
'Soldier and Witch', figure, 94
Solon, Marc Louis, 10
Soroe School, Denmark, 85
Spode, 67, 68, 84
Staehr-Nielsen, Eva, 124, 149a
Staffordshire, 84
Stanley, C. F., 72
'Star' pattern, 63, 67
Stephensen, Snorre, 134, 149a
Stoneware, 96ff, 104-111
Stosch, Philippe de, 39, 41
Stouenberg, 49
Strohblume (immortelle), 58, 63
Struensee, John Frederik, 18
Style pittoresque, 21, 31
Sumeria, 10
Sung dynasty, wares and glazes, 57, 96, 124
Svardalyn, J., 149a

Svardalyn, Raben, 24, 148a
Swan Service, Meissen, 21, 51
Sweden, Danish treaty with, 44
'Swineherd', figure, 94
Switzerland, 57
Syria, 61

T

T'ang dynasty, 57
Temmoku wares, 104
'Tenera' range, 124
Thirty Years' War, 21
Thomaschevsky, Carl Friedrich, 24, 148a
Thomsen, Chr., 92n, 94, 149a
Thorrson, Nils, 110, 124, 131, 149a
Thorvaldsen, Bertel, 85
Thorvaldsen Museum, 118
Thuringia, porcelain of, 57, 63
Tidsskrift for Kunstindustri, quoted 94, 96n
Tiffany, Louis, 100
Tilskueren, 92
Times, The, quoted 10
Ting wares, see Sung
Toshiro (Shunkei), 96
Tranquebar Service, 132
'Transmutation' glazes, 100
Triton service, 134
Trolle, Anne-Marie, 124, 134, 149a
Tvede, Claus, 24, 72, 148a

V

Van Gogh, Vincent, 96
Vasegaard, Gertrude, 134
Venice, 12
Vestergaard, Sven, 28
Victoria and Albert Museum, 50, 77, 100, and in notes and captions throughout
Vienna Porcelain Manufactory, 14, 21, 84, 85
Vincennes (later Sèvres), 13, 15n
'Virgin paste', 31, 37, 66
Vogt, Georges, 100, 107, 110
Vort Land, quoted 50

W

Washington, George, see American War of Independence
Watney, Bernard, 57n, 60n
Wedgwood, family, 13, 105n
Wedgwood, Enoch, 63
Wedgwood, Josiah, 27, 31, 41n, 44
Wedgwood, Josiah C., 13n, 84n
Weiss, Ivan, 110, 124, 149a
Whistler, J. A. McNeill, 87

Whiter, Leonard, 67
Wiedewelt, Johannes, 14, 72n, 79
Wilde, Oscar, 87
Wilkins, W. H., 18n
Williamson, Dr G. C., 44n
Willow pattern, 57
Winckelmann, Johann J., 84
Windsor Castle, see Alexandra, Princess
Wolstrup, Matthias, 24
Wood family, Staffordshire, 84
Worcester Royal Porcelain Manufactory, 60, 121
Worsaae, J. J. A., 50n

Y

Yao, Chinese ware, 12
Ying ch'ing (or *ch'ing pai*), white Sung wares, 57
Yüan dynasty, 12, 56, 57
Yule, Sir Henry, quoted 12

Z

Zwiebelmuster ('Onion' pattern), 57
Zurich Porcelain Manufactory, 60